a call to Grace

david nasser author of a call to die

david nasser | author of a call to die

Published by Redemptive Art Publishing
Printed by Rose Printing

Printed in the United States of America

ISBN: 978-0-9792479-2-7

Designed by LeAnn Gentry

I want to thank...

Jesus Christ; our Grace and Truth.

Jennifer, there is no one else's hand I would rather hold. I adore you. Thanks for all the hard work that you put into these pages. Writing at Seaside was surreal.

Rudy and Grace, you are my heart, my squeezy squeezies.

The Nasser, Davis, and Morgan families. Especially my football buddies, Emmanuel and Benjamin. I love you tremendously.

Our hard-working, committed staff family: Dana Davis, Amelia Ann Davis, Justin Terry, Amanda Humphries, Cathy Barnes, and Jason Bowman.

Our amazingly supportive board of directors: Phil Newberry, Bob Thompson, Bill Greer, Dennis Rogers, Bill Sones, Joel Engle, and Steve Richardson.

The greatest friends that anyone could ask for; the Davis's, the Clements, the Engles, the Himayas, the Petersons, the Underwoods, the Gills, the Powells, the Stanleys, the Stracks, Francis, the Satterfields, the Halls, and the Bozemans.

My pastor, Buddy Gray, and the great staff at Hunter Street Baptist Church.

Our partners in ministry: Student Life, Billy Graham Evangelistic Association, LifeWay, North American Mission Board, Student Leadership University, Youth Specialties, The Scott Dawson Association, Chuck Tilley, Xtreme Conferences, Word Made Flesh, Christ in Youth, C-Kruis, Redeem the Vote, Merch Plaza, Million Man March, Enfuego, Jim Newberry, all of the festivals that partner with us, LeAnn Gentry, John Foulk, Rose Printing, Peter Harrill, InQuest Ministries, Georgia Baptist Youth Ministries, Vertical Ministries, World Vision, ICTA (keep serving), Mike Love, Premier Productions, Third Day (still the best, baby), Chris Tomlin and band (earn the shirt), MercyMe (Bart, thanks for the call to Jeff), Audio A (for dedicating "Big House"), Big Daddy Weave (my bus you're on), Salvador (for Spanish songs to Rudy—gracias!), Todd Agnew (shoeless wonder), the Barlow family (I'm a Barlow boy), Building 429 (no more pranks, I promise), Starfield (thanks for the song 'ay!), By the Tree (finally paid), Shane and Shane (can't wait till tour).

The many authors who have inspired these words and who have written books that have changed my life from one of duty to one of delight. Thank you for the many quotes. I wish I could write half as well...

Last but not least, the *masterpieces* who made up the portraits of grace. Thank you for letting me tell your stories. And of course the BNCC.

Soli Deo Gloria!

Table of contents

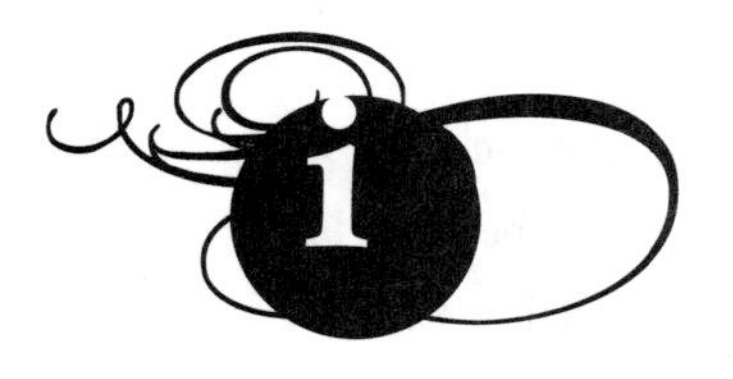

Introduction

How can this be?

I remember the moment it happened. I was sitting alone on the pontoon boat floor. It was a very hot Monday afternoon in May, and the wind was gusting. When *it* happened, I stood up and shouted as loud as I have ever shouted. I just didn't know how else to respond. I felt like a lightning rod that had finally been struck. "How can this be?" I kept screaming over and over again. "How can this be?"

That hot, windy afternoon, God brought me face to face with his grace. His gentle, yet powerful, life-changing grace.

I had taken a few days' sabbatical to go to my in-laws' house. Jennifer's parents live on a lake in the country. The kind of place where you can grab a cup of coffee and sit on the porch, completely secluded. Or maybe, as I did, take a boat ride alone. *Alone* is a rare treasure in my life. It's an opportunity to shut up and listen. By the way, having learned from experience, I'll tell you: never miss an opportunity to shut up and listen!

I had been by myself three days; reading and meditating. It was on the last morning I decided to get on the pontoon boat with just my Bible. Since I am slightly ADDD (attention deficit disorder deliberately!), sometimes I need help to stay focused. So in the very middle of the lake, I sat with my Bible open to Ephesians 2:8. It had taken my entire sabbatical time to go from Ephesians 1:1 to Ephesians 2:7. That might seem like a snail's pace to some, but I felt I was truly rushing. My intent was to take slow sips and not big gulps, savoring every single word. Suddenly, there it was, in all its glory: "For by grace you have been saved through faith. And this is not your own doing; it is the gift of God" (Ephesians 2:8).

I already knew the verse by memory, but not "by heart." It wasn't a new declaration for me, but definitely a new revelation. What a revolutionary truth—the gift of grace. The fact that God loves unlovable me based not on the good or the bad I do but on his unmerited favor. This was truly mind blowing to me. This reality was bigger than big! Sure, I had heard sermons and read books about God's grace. I had even preached about it myself. But God, in that moment, confronted me with the fact that although I might have believed in his grace, and even received it, I had not fallen madly in love with it. In all actuality, I had taken amazing grace and replaced it with amazing works. I had created a list of dos and don'ts, and had become quite efficient at checking them off, one by one.

I had bought the lie that the same grace that saved me was not strong enough to sustain me. But I didn't stop there. I had taken my list and turned it into sermons built around earning the gift. Although I never preached that literally, looking back I realize I did unintentionally preach it. In my heart, I was accomplishing what I thought God wanted me to do. *God can't possibly mean that grace is totally free, right?* I thought. A totally free grace sounded weak and frail. I rationalized, *You know, Lord, if I really preached about a completely free grace, it will give Christians license to sin, won't it? If I tell people that grace is absolutely free, won't it cheapen the sacrifice Jesus made on the cross?*

Frankly, works worked for me because I spent so much time calling the church to do more and to try harder. That kind of preaching always seemed to have an immediate effect. A works-driven life looked just as good as a grace-driven one, except it was easier on the ego, and it produced results. My message was usually more about sin management than it was about walking in grace. It got people moving either down the aisle or to the product tables. Either way, it was good for "business." Grace alone seemed to be a message that was way too passive. I would tell you in a second that salvation was a free gift, but if you kept listening, my interpretation described a gift with strings attached. Sure, I believed we are all saved by grace. But, at the end of the day, grace was a Trojan horse; a gift with a hidden agenda.

That was the reason I kept shouting, "How could it be?" that day on the boat. I was a ten-year-old Christian in the ministry, and in my attempts not to cheapen grace, I had actually done just that. I was involuntarily calling people to legalism and religion, instead of to a life of freedom and victory that only grace can offer. That Monday morning on the pontoon boat, God called me to *stop doing and start being:* to stop preaching about doing and to start preaching about being. Christianity is not about doing godly things to earn God's grace, but about being godly because we already have God's grace. Grace is a free gift. There are no strings attached. It's not about my behavior, but about my identity. Sure we're called to do, but we are called to do as we be, *not* do in order to be! If you're thinking right now, *What in the world is he talking about?* don't worry. My intent is to make these theological cookies bite-size. I will attempt to put these nuggets of truth on the bottom shelf using humor and easy-to-understand language. I hope you'll get it.

Anyway, back to my story, I got off the boat and headed home. I called Jennifer to check in. I hadn't talked to her for three days, and she was five months pregnant with our little girl.

"How was your sabbatical? I'm dying to hear all about it. Can you just give me a hint about the things God has said to you?" she inquired.

I immediately stated, "God gave me the name of our daughter."

With a little apprehension she said, "And..."

With certainty, I replied, "Grace."

Since that day, my greatest passion has been to boldly proclaim the grace and truth of God. Grace hasn't softened the message of the gospel; instead it has empowered it. The message of grace calls God's people to new heights of obedience and responsibility. Surprisingly, I find myself in a little more hot water these days. In many cases, the church today has a hard time embracing the grace-full life. We're often more comfortable embracing a duty-full one. Many times as Christians, we feel better when we're doing stuff for God, as if we could pay him back, or at least somehow earn his love. With that kind of religious mentality running wild, the message of grace is controversial and scandalous to say the least.

During the next thirty-nine days, we are going to dive into Ephesians 2:1-10. (By the way, if you're wondering, *Why thirty-nine days?* I had set out to write a forty-day devotional, but when it was all said and done, it came out to thirty-nine days. It was as if God was saying to me, *"Let it go. I told you this was supposed to be a book about grace."* As we look at the grace of God, and how Christianity is not about doing, but being, you might get uncomfortable at times. All that I ask is that you stay the course. Don't just read some of this book; read it all. To play Russian roulette and randomly read parts here and there is to run the risk of this book sounding legalistic at one moment and liberal at another. Hear me out. I pray that as you take the entire journey, you will see the obvious balance.

Warning: The grace-driven life is addictive and highly contagious. Listen! Can you hear him calling? It's a call to grace...

Grace gear

Features to help you with your 39-day journey

1. Ephesians 2:1-10 is printed at the beginning of each reading. This will hopefully help you as you strive to burn these words into your heart.
2. Discussion questions at the end of each reading will help solidify the information you just learned.
3. At the end of each day, there are the same three journal entries. One deals with how God may be *convicting* you. Another focuses on how God may be *comforting* and assuring you. The last journal entry asks how God may be *calling* you to apply the information you are learning.
4. Every four days I have inserted a Portrait of Grace. These are basically mini biographies of some very average saints of God who have, through Christ, overcome tremendous circumstances and become masterpieces of God's grace. As a follow-up to each portrait, I have created what I call a Grace Extension. This is a practical way to reach out and extend grace to others who might be in a similar situation as the person you've just read about. There's no more beautiful way to practice living in God's grace than to find ways to extend it to others. I have purposefully tried to think of ways to take us all out of our comfort zone. In fact, I don't believe grace even has a comfort zone.

Some ideas provided are easy to complete and take little time. Some require more time and effort and cannot be completed in the four-day time span before the next Grace Extension. I encourage you to take time loving on these people. You may feel a little silly approaching some of these Grace Extensions. You might get a little messy in the process, and all the loose ends may not be tied together neatly by the end of the journey. That's OK. That's usually how grace operates. I like to think that's probably how God wants it.

Please be free with this. Love lavishly. Love foolishly. You're probably way more creative than I am, so use your imagination—create fresher, bigger opportunities than I've suggested to you. You may want to get together with some friends in your Sunday school class or youth group, and together extend grace to a whole group of people. Go for it! Give your grace theology some unique hands and feet!

Grace guide

How to get the most out of this book

We live in a microwaveable world. We put popcorn in, push the "popcorn" button (because we don't have the time to punch in all the numbers), and three minutes later, it's ready to eat. Even when it comes to microwave popcorn we stand there, tap our feet, look at our watch and wonder, *How long is this going to take?!* In these days everything exists at DSL speed. We want everything *now.* No, that's not even good enough. We want it yesterday.

In our "I want it yesterday" society, it is extremely rare to slow down, take our time, and adopt a "crock-pot" mentality concerning anything in our lives. Well, I will ask you to do just that. For the next thirty-nine days, slow down! Allow this book to take you on a daily journey, not a ten-second sprint. Allow God's grace to slowly seep into your pores. The reading will focus your mind on his grace. The journaling will place his grace on your heart. Then the Grace Extensions will direct your feet and hands to demonstrate his grace. My sincere prayer is that by tasting God's grace, drop by daily drop over the following thirty-nine days, your soul will be left with a thirst that only more of his grace can satisfy.

The following suggestions will help you learn more about God's grace and how to most effectively use this book:

1. Make this journey with God a priority for the next thirty-nine days. Begin your day with the readings, questions, and scripture memorization. You may want to save the journal entries for the end of the evening. This will allow time to meditate on what God revealed to you that morning and throughout the day. One practical way to make this work is to get up thirty minutes earlier. I have learned that if I start my day with scripture and prayer, I am more capable of handling the curve balls that life may throw at me during the day.
2. Come up with inventive ways to memorize the ten verses of scripture. Each daily

reading begins with the first ten verses from Ephesians 2. Don't skip this. Read it every day. Write it down. Take index cards with the verses written out to practice the verses at lunch, or even write them on your bathroom mirror. Do what you need to do to hide these words in your heart.

3. Make notes, highlight, underline, insert your name—do whatever it takes to personalize this book and to personalize what God is teaching you about his grace. Apply it. Marinate in it. Own it.
4. I challenge you to fast for the next thirty-nine days. Fasting is spiritual concentration. In this case, I'm asking you to substitute an unnecessary daily activity for extra time with God. Before you dive in, ask God what you should fast from. Chances are, you already know.
5. Use the journaling time not only for reflection and writing but also for prayer. Keep the lines of communication open between you and God. Let your prayer time become a launching pad to express in writing what God is teaching you.

1

Small

"And you were dead in the trespasses and sins in which you once walked, following the course of this world, following the prince of the power of the air, the spirit that is now at work in the sons of disobedience—among whom we all once lived in the passions of our flesh, carrying out the desires of the body and the mind, and were by nature children of wrath, like the rest of mankind. But God, being rich in mercy, because of the great love with which he loved us, even when we were dead in our trespasses, made us alive together with Christ—by grace you have been saved—and raised us up with him and seated us with him in the heavenly places in Christ Jesus, so that in the coming ages he might show the immeasurable riches of his grace in kindness toward us in Christ Jesus. For by grace you have been saved through faith. And this is not your own doing; it is the gift of God, not a result of works, so that no one may boast. For we are his workmanship, created in Christ Jesus for good works, which God prepared beforehand, that we should walk in them."
(Ephesians 2:1-10)

Become who you are. These four words can encapsulate not only the main message of this book but everything the apostle Paul spent his time and energy calling the people of Ephesus to be. Before we begin looking at Ephesians 2:1-10, it will help to understand a little about its author, Paul. Knowing a little about the man who penned the passages will help the words have a greater impact on our lives.

Paul's letter to the people of Ephesus is not just spouting out good theological ideas, but giving a testimony of the grace Paul has experienced himself. As in many of his letters, Paul begins Ephesians by identifying himself: "Paul, an apostle of Christ Jesus by the will of God, to the saints who are in Ephesus, and are faithful in Christ Jesus." Paul. At its very definition, the name *Paul* means "small." This is quite ironic considering that Paul is arguably the most quoted man not just in all of Christianity but in all of history. Think of the hundreds of thousands of people in pulpits every Sunday around the world, opening a Bible and quoting the apostle Paul. Think of the wives who write an encouragement by Paul to a husband who is serving in a war somewhere. Think of the husband who claims out loud a scripture written by Paul to help his wife during labor. Think of the much-worn youth camp T-shirt that sports a verse from the book of Romans across the front. Considering all this, the last thing that would come to mind is to associate the apostle Paul with the word *small.*

But in fact, that is exactly how Paul wanted to be thought of. Everything about him is reduced; everything about Christ is exalted. I don't think Paul ever set out writing these letters thinking, *Oh, the royalty checks I will receive from these!* or, *I'll definitely outsell Harry Potter and The Atkins Diet.* As a matter of fact, I'm sure Paul realized, even while writing these letters, that they were not his words. Think about it. He was merely the megaphone that the Holy Spirit used not only to speak to the first-century Christians but also to transcend time and speak to us today. Paul titles himself "a *servant* of the gospel" (Eph. 3:7). Note again that he is not a *celebrity,* but a *servant.* In Romans 1:1, he describes himself again, "Paul, a servant of Christ Jesus, called to be an apostle, set apart for the gospel of God."

It is obvious when you hang out in any of his letters, with Ephesians being no exception, Paul is not speaking down to the reader, "Look at all I have accomplished, being the big, righteous celebrity," but saying, "Look at all God has done through me." Maybe that is why God has allowed his letters and his life to continue to have a rippling effect in our lives so many centuries later. God uses Paul's writings not to make much of Paul but to make much of himself. In the day and age of "Christian celebrities," who fight for real estate on the shelves of Christian bookstores, it is refreshing to be reminded that Paul was all about the only true famous one, Jesus Christ.

As we look at Paul's life, let's make sure we honor him by keeping him small and not getting so caught up in the messenger that we miss the message. As a side note, know that the first three devotionals are shorter in length on purpose. This way you can spend more time familiarizing yourself with the pace. Use these extra moments to develop a routine of meditation, prayer, and scripture memory. As the days go by, you will be able to take the "training wheels" off and just go for it.

Be Still. Listen to what God is saying to you.

1. Go back and reread the first sentence of this chapter, "Become who you are." Think about this statement. Are there any areas of your life where *what you do* contradicts *who you are*?

2. In your own words, describe how you attempt to earn God's favor or win his approval.

3. What are some things that this society does to make us think "bigger is better"?

4. Why does God often use the "small" to accomplish his will? (Hint: Read 1 Corinthians 1:27-29.) How does the reality of "small" directly impact your life?

5. Is there anything in your life that you are doing to make your name big instead of God's name?

Lord, I thank you that today your grace is *comforting* me in these areas:

Lord, I thank you that today your grace is *convicting* me in these areas:

Lord, I thank you that today your grace is *calling* me to:

Today's Memory Verse: Ephesians 2:1

When in Rome...

"And you were dead in the trespasses and sins in which you once walked, following the course of this world, following the prince of the power of the air, the spirit that is now at work in the sons of disobedience—among whom we all once lived in the passions of our flesh, carrying out the desires of the body and the mind, and were by nature children of wrath, like the rest of mankind. But God, being rich in mercy, because of the great love with which he loved us, even when we were dead in our trespasses, made us alive together with Christ—by grace you have been saved—and raised us up with him and seated us with him in the heavenly places in Christ Jesus, so that in the coming ages he might show the immeasurable riches of his grace in kindness toward us in Christ Jesus. For by grace you have been saved through faith. And this is not your own doing; it is the gift of God, not a result of works, so that no one may boast. For we are his workmanship, created in Christ Jesus for good works, which God prepared beforehand, that we should walk in them."

(Ephesians 2:1-10)

A few years ago in Rome, I got into a cab. I had been there for three days with a list of places I wanted to see. I was there for personal reflection, however, my moments of reflection had gone overtime to the point that I was running like crazy trying to finish my list. In my own defense, it is hard not to lose track of time when staring at the magnificence of the Sistine Chapel, or contemplating the bloodshed and suffering endured by fellow believers two thousand years ago at the Coliseum.

Anyway, I jumped into the cab and the driver immediately assumed I was Italian. This is when it all began to go south: Instead of letting the cab driver know I am indeed not Italian, flattery got the best of me. I hid my geeky tourist map (which I could have used to ensure I got to the right place), and instead, with the best Italian accent I could muster, I proceeded to say, *"Sanpaulobasilca."* (Think of Tony from *Who's the Boss?*) What I was trying to say was, "Please take me to the church called *Saint Peter in Chains*," a famous place where the actual chains used to keep Peter in prison are displayed. What I actually said was some Italian sounding gibberish that included the word *Paul* and not the word *Peter*. The man looked back at me, somewhat confused, and said a couple of sentences in Italian. But again, instead of pulling out my map like a good little tourist should, I confidently grinned and yelled out, *"Sí!"*

Fifty minutes later I was dropped off in a part of town that, in fact, did not feel like a part of any town at all. The cab driver dropped me off at a church very appropriately named Saint Paul's Outside the Walls. What an understatement! I was beginning to wonder if we were even still in Italy or if I needed to get out my map of Switzerland. My first impression of this church was, *This can't possibly be a very important place to see if it is not even on my list, and it has no lines and no admission price.* I couldn't have been more wrong. Normally, I might say at this point something about God taking lemons and making lemonade, but I was in Rome—so I guess God was about to take sour grapes and make sweet wine. (For the Baptist folks, it was unfermented!!)

Saint Paul's Outside the Walls is a basilica (church) with thirty-six frescos of the life of Paul. In the old days, most people were illiterate and artists would paint biblical scenes on the walls of churches so that the everyday man could experience scripture. So for the next four hours I sat with my Bible turned to Acts chapter nine and meditated on these painted walls. Three and a half of those four hours were spent pondering the first and second paintings only, while the last thiry minutes were spent looking at the other thirty-four.

The apostle Paul had a very colorful life. From Luke's writings in Acts, we know he began as a very devout Jew named Saul. He even referred to himself as a "Jew of Jews." He was so devout, in fact, that he persecuted Christians and even participated in the stoning death of the apostle, Stephen. On the road to Damascus, a bright light from heaven blinded Paul and a voice (Jesus) thundered, "Saul, Saul, why are you persecuting me?" (Acts 9:4). After three days of blindness, Saul surrendered his life to the Lord, and later became known as Paul. He became the voice of God to the Gentiles (everyone who is not Jewish), and went through many experiences in his life before being martyred.

What got me stuck between the first and second frescos was the obvious contrast between the two. In the first painting, Paul is illustrated as an accomplice to murder. He is looking down with a glare of approval and pleasure as Stephen is being stoned. It is seen in his eyes. Stare at the painting long enough and it comes alive—I felt Paul's intent to kill Stephen. Paul's hand is ready on his sword.

What made Paul so angry was not that Stephen had come and crashed his keg party with a big "What Would Jesus Do?" message, or even that Stephen had told Paul to live a more religious life by dumping his girlfriend. That wasn't the case at all. In fact, Paul was a Jewish scholar who attempted to keep all the laws and wanted to see God honored and obeyed. With 613 commands passed down from God to his people, Paul was all about obeying the laws to the fullest extent, in order to earn God's approval. Paul believed that by obeying all the law he could earn his own salvation. Ultimately he couldn't, but his checklist of dos and don'ts looked a lot better than the lists of those around him.

Enter Stephen. Stephen's message confronted Paul with the truth of the gospel. This infuriated Paul because, in essence, Stephen was saying, "Hey Paul, you may feel really good about your to-do list, but your very best is still not good enough." Stephen's message was simple: You are having trouble obeying all the Jewish law. Well, guess what? Jesus is the "newish" law. How'd you like them apples!? For example, if the Jewish law says do not commit adultery, the "newish" law says that if you even consider adultery in your mind, you are guilty whether you practice it or not. You thought you were in trouble because you couldn't fulfill all 613 commands—*GOOD NEWS!* You are in a whole lot more trouble than you think you're in.

This scenario was so beautifully depicted in the first fresco. Stephen is on his knees, hands spread to heaven in a posture of worship as he is being stoned to death. The artist didn't hold back—you see bloody stones on the ground, angry legalists looking for bigger rocks, and Paul standing over Stephen as if to say, *"Your Jesus has brought you to your knees to die."* I found myself despising Paul in this scene, yet at the same time, identifying with him. I, too, used to look at the "Stephens" of the world with disdain, while in arrogance I prided myself in all the laws I had kept. To be angry with Paul in this first fresco is to be angry at who, I used to be: not someone *with* Christ but *against* Christ.

Be Still. Listen to what God is saying to you.

1. Have you ever witnessed or heard of someone being persecuted for what he believed?

   Describe what happened and how you felt.

2. Be honest. Have you ever persecuted or made fun of someone because they were outspoken about their faith?

3. Have you ever been persecuted or made fun of for what you believe? Describe what happened and how you felt.

4. Think back to a time in your life when a movie scene, a painting, or even something in nature brought God's truth to life for you. Describe that moment and the truth that was made clear.

Lord, I thank you that today your grace is *comforting* me in these areas:

Lord, I thank you that today your grace is *convicting* me in these areas:

Lord, I thank you that today your grace is *calling* me to:

Today's Memory Verse: Ephesians 2:1

One step to the right

"And you were dead in the trespasses and sins in which you once walked, following the course of this world, following the prince of the power of the air, the spirit that is now at work in the sons of disobedience—among whom we all once lived in the passions of our flesh, carrying out the desires of the body and the mind, and were by nature children of wrath, like the rest of mankind. But God, being rich in mercy, because of the great love with which he loved us, even when we were dead in our trespasses, made us alive together with Christ—by grace you have been saved—and raised us up with him and seated us with him in the heavenly places in Christ Jesus, so that in the coming ages he might show the immeasurable riches of his grace in kindness toward us in Christ Jesus. For by grace you have been saved through faith. And this is not your own doing; it is the gift of God, not a result of works, so that no one may boast. For we are his workmanship, created in Christ Jesus for good works, which God prepared beforehand, that we should walk in them." (Ephesians 2:1-10)

Yesterday we talked about the first fresco at *"Sanpaulobasilca."* Today, take one step to the right. Literally, that is the number of steps it took to get from Pietro Cavallini's first fresco to his second fresco there in that sanctuary.

The second painting finds Paul on the Damascus Road—with beautiful irony, in the same physical posture as Stephen in the first fresco—bowed down before the heavens. Chills will run down your spine when you realize that the same man who stood against Christ now finds himself brought to his knees, face to face with Jesus. This is the moment of Paul's conversion. The one step to the right should remind us that the story is not over. If there had only been the one painting, we would simply see a portrait of Paul, the first great persecutor of the church. But the physical step to the right represents a comma, not a period. It's the "I once was lost, but now I'm found" moment that takes the enemy of the gospel and turns him into a friend of God. The first painting is a tragedy as it pertains to Paul's life. But suddenly, (Acts 9:1) with one quick step to the right, we see everything change.

Do you remember your Damascus Road? I was eighteen years, two months old, and like Paul, everything in my life symbolically breathed out "murderous threats" against Christ. The "Stephens" in my life were teenagers in a local youth group who confronted me with the truth of who I really was. Even though I was a stone thrower, it was on a Saturday night in my bedroom when suddenly a light from heaven flashed around me. No, I'm not saying this was a physical light as with Paul. It wasn't my physical eyes God opened, but the eyes of my heart. I, like Paul, came to the realization, through the Holy Spirit, that there is nothing I could do in my own strength to earn salvation. I had to trust Christ and Christ alone. As Paul and I both learned, it is about not what I can *do*, but what Christ has already *done.*

As we explore Ephesians chapter two over the next thiry-seven days, it is helpful to remind ourselves that Paul is shouting about grace at the top of his lungs because his own life is a testimony of God's unmerited favor. When Paul writes about going from death to life in Ephesians 2:1, it is because he has personally experienced spiritual death and resurrection. When Paul expounds on the free gift of grace in Ephesians 2:4, it is because he personally received it. And when Paul talks about becoming a masterpiece for the glory of God in Ephesians 2:10, it is because his own life became just that.

By the way, if you're wondering about the remaining thirty-four frescos in Saint Paul's Outside the Walls, they are thirty-four masterpieces that beautifully reflect the incredible workmanship Paul's life became once God took him one step to the right.

Be Still. Listen to what God is saying to you.

1. Go back in time and think of a situation in which you believed you were right, and then later realized how wrong you really were. Describe how you reacted as you saw the truth.

2. Has there ever been a moment in your life when, like Paul, you were boldly confronted with the truth of Jesus Christ? Describe that experience.

3. Can you remember a time when someone stretched out a hand of grace to you, although you in no way deserved it?

4. How can you extend grace to someone in your life that seems undeserving?

Lord, I thank you that today your grace is *comforting* me in these areas:

Lord, I thank you that today your grace is *convicting* me in these areas:

Lord, I thank you that today your grace is *calling* me to:

Today's Memory Verse: Ephesians 2:1

A Beautiful Mess

I know that a lot of times it is hard for a man to admit when another man is better looking than he is, but I'm secure enough in my masculinity to say that Greg Howard is a good-looking fella. At one time in his life he was paid a lot of money because of his perfect jawbone structure! Whatever.

During his last year of college, Greg was dating a local model and often went along to her photo shoots. An agent approached him at a shoot one day and asked him if he had ever modeled. Greg started doing some modeling work, and it wasn't long before his career skyrocketed; he relocated to New York and worked with the Ford Modeling Agency. For people in the modeling world, this is about as big as it gets. Almost immediately, the agency sent him to Paris. The pace of life in Paris was nothing like he had growing up, but he quickly adjusted. Greg earned lots of money and enjoyed spending it on parties, traveling, and gorgeous women.

He moved back to the U.S. after two years in Paris, and the lifestyle he had been living just intensified. Making money, partying, and achieving fame were top on Greg's "to do" list, and he was rapidly meeting his goals. Greg commuted between New York and Miami, invested in a nightclub, and was totally committed to fueling his outwardly glamorous lifestyle. However, Greg says he knew deep down that one day it was somehow all going to catch up with him.

That "one day" came sooner than he thought. As Greg entered his home one night, he noticed the blinking message light on his telephone. One of his best friends in New York had left an urgent message, and Greg immediately called him back. The friend quickly told Greg that his ex-live-in girlfriend had just died of AIDS. Greg was in complete shock. He thought, *How could this have happened?* With his emotions in an uproar, he couldn't see a way out. He felt as if he had just been sentenced to death. His friends in the modeling business tried to offer their support, but none of them offered any kind of hope.

The things in Greg's life that had once seemed important were all of a sudden empty and meaningless. He didn't know where to turn since none of his friends could really help. He had no desire to tell his parents, because he was afraid of the worry and social stigma it would bring to their lives.

Greg finally worked up the nerve to get tested for HIV. The wait for results was an agonizing week and a half. He hoped as he returned to the clinic, that this was all a dream, until the nurse handed him a piece of paper that was titled "FOR THOSE WHO HAVE TESTED POSITIVE FOR THE HIV VIRUS." Greg sat hopeless and realized none of the things he had tried to achieve in his life (career, fame, friends, money) could help him now. Jesus tells us in Mark 8:36-37, "For what does it profit a man to gain the whole world and forfeit his life? For what can a man give in return for his life?"

Greg was so lost and scared that he began desperately searching for answers. One Sunday morning as he channel-surfed, he landed on a TV church service. Greg thought, *Hey, maybe I should give church a shot.* He called a friend who attended church and asked if he could join him sometime. Greg recalled he was annoyed at first with the style of his friend's contemporary church, but as the service went on, something began to stir in his soul. The Holy Spirit began to work in Greg. God's message to Greg was one of his complete love and forgiveness. Greg began to understand Jesus' willingness to meet Greg right where he was in the middle of all the pain, anger, and fear. That day at church, all of Greg's initial annoyance evaporated and he surrendered his broken, messed-up life into God's hands. He began to cry and could not stop. One thing that was so powerful to Greg was that this church didn't condemn him, but instead extended grace. Romans 2:4 is true when it says that it is God's kindness that leads us to repentance.

God instantly began to transform Greg. His taste buds were no longer tuned to the life he was used to. The things he used to love, he now hated; and the things he once hated, he now loved. He got out of the nightclub business and completely quit the party scene. He became involved in Bible study and church fellowship. For the first time in his life, Greg experienced true abundance in life, even though he was in the toughest place he had ever been.

Today, Greg is still living with HIV. He is married to a godly woman who serves with him in full-time ministry. Yes, full-time ministry. Greg Howard is the youth and college pastor at one of the largest churches in the country. His life is such a strong picture of the miracle of God's grace. Did God take Greg's disease away? No. But God has taken the sickness that will eventually rob Greg of his life and is using it as a platform to display his glory and the sufficiency of his grace to all of us who struggle with the sins of the past. God's grace can not only erase the past but also build a new future. Greg's testimony demonstrates that not only is God's grace enough during times when on top of the world, but it is also enough in the lowest valley.

The Lord is always quick to forgive, and slow to anger, abounding in love. When all the circumstances in our lives seem like shifting sand, and we have nothing tangible to grab on to, we are reminded over and over in the Psalms that it is God's love that is steadfast, immovable, and never changing. Greg's story shows that God is never through with us, and we should never be through with our fellow brothers and sisters in Christ. God's grace gives us all the power to truly overcome the past, to endure the present, and to prepare for the future.

I'll never forget sitting there listening to Greg's story, thinking of how God continues to take tragedy and turn it into testimony. Greg concluded, "I thank God every day that I'm HIV positive. If it hadn't been for that, I wouldn't be here today."

Grace Extension

Greg Howard is among the many co-laborers in God's army who serve faithfully day in and day out. When God called Greg into the ministry, he was called to a life of long nights and early mornings. To label the job of someone on a church staff "full-time" is a serious understatement. The demands on a minister's life usually take their toll not only on the minister but on his family as well. This is why today's Grace Extension is a call to serve God's servants. Think about someone you know on a church staff who could really use a break. Get together with others from your church group and make plans to give this servant and spouse a night out. A few can be in charge of baby-sitting, while a few go out to buy movie tickets and a gift certificate for dinner. If you really want to go all out, you can even throw in the element of surprise by cleaning the house, washing the car, raking the leaves, etc. while they are away at dinner. If you're the solo grace extender, then just show up on a Saturday morning and cut the grass for your pastor to allow him time to watch Saturday-morning cartoons with his grandchildren. If none of these work in your particular church staff situation, then tailor-make this Grace Extension to work with your circumstances. Remember that grace is unmerited, with no strings attached. So when you extend grace, you are not expecting anything in return. The blessing is that you get to be the one who blesses.

Be Involved!

Today's Memory Verses: Ephesians 2:1-2

Lord, I thank you that today your grace is *comforting* me in these areas:

Lord, I thank you that today your grace is *convicting* me in these areas:

Lord, I thank you that today your grace is *calling* me to:

Today's Memory Verse: Ephesians 2:1-2

You were

*"**And you were** dead in the trespasses and sins in which you once walked, following the prince of the power of the air, the spirit that is now at work in the sons of disobedience—among whom we all once lived in the passions of our flesh, carrying out the desires of the body and the mind, and were by nature children of wrath, like the rest of mankind. But God, being rich in mercy, because of the great love with which he loved us, even when we were dead in our trespasses, made us alive together with Christ—by grace you have been saved—and raised us up with him and seated us with him in the heavenly places in Christ Jesus, so that in the coming ages he might show the immeasurable riches of his grace in kindness toward us in Christ Jesus. For by grace you have been saved through faith. And this is not your own doing; it is the gift of God, not a result of works, so that no one may boast. For we are his workmanship, created in Christ Jesus for good works, which God prepared beforehand, that we should walk in them."*

(Ephesians 2:1-10)

The night I became a Christian, one of the first things I did was call a man whom I considered to be instrumental in my coming to faith in Christ. I can't remember exactly what time it was, but suffice it to say, it was well past bedtime. I remember his sleepy voice as I shared with him how I had bowed a knee in my room and asked Christ to save me. There were a lot of encouraging things said in that conversation, but something that has always stuck out to me was the phrase "You're in the boat now." He explained how I had been drowning in a sea of sin and every time I tried to come up for air, my sin kept dragging me down. But on that night, God came by in his boat. (I figure that if it was God's boat it must have been the Love Boat!) God saw me drowning and threw out the lifesaver—Jesus. My friend explained that I had symbolically grabbed the lifesaver and God had pulled me into the boat.

Since then, I have heard that illustration several times and I am convinced it is always shared with good intentions from great people. However, when you look at Ephesians 2:1, Paul does not say that we are *drowning* in our sins, but that we have *already drowned.* This is where we must all begin, at the end of ourselves. In Ephesians 2:1, Paul clearly states that you and I are dead in our transgressions and sins.

And *you...*

Paul begins with the word *you.* Although he is

speaking to the people of Ephesus, those words are just as true and relevant to every single person today. *You* means everyone. You can take the word *you* out and insert the names David Nasser, or Billy Graham, or Marilyn Manson, or any other name for that matter, and the verse still applies to each person throughout history. None of us is exempt. Romans 3:23 says, "For *all* have sinned and fall short of the glory of God" (emphasis added).

...you *were...*

The next word is *were.* Paul says that every single one of us was dead in our trespasses and sins. It is important to note here that he is talking to the saints, those who are already believers. Much like himself and every one of us, this is what we were, not what we are. But God didn't leave us that way. Great hope can be found in the word *were.* Just because that's what we *were*, doesn't mean that's what we *are*.

In the mid-1800s, with the South still in the midst of slavery, a couple generations of Africans had already been born in the United States knowing nothing except the bondage of slavery. Then one day, slavery was abolished.

The abolition of slavery made many slave owners hit the roof—literally. I can just see them climbing on top of their roofs, all over the South, gathering all their slaves together, and giving them a speech. I imagine the speeches must have gone something like this:

"You might have heard that you have been set free. But let me ask you a question: do you feel like you're free? Of course you don't. Your mama was a slave. Your daddy was a slave, and you have never been anything but a slave! Look at you. You're dressed like a slave, you have blisters like a slave, and all your life you have taken orders from me. Today is no different. Now, get back to work."

I can see the whip in his hand. Tragically, many slaves believed the lies. Even though they were completely free, many continued to live and work as slaves. That's who they *were*. That's all they thought they could ever be.

I love to imagine, though, that maybe one day, a tired old slave finally threw down his shovel, possibly with the thought, *My back hurts and my neck is burned from the sun, but I'm no longer the slave I feel like I am. That's who I was. The president said I was free. That's not how I feel, but it's who I am now. I'm gonna be who I am, and not who I was.* I can hear his cries, louder and louder, as he yelled across the hot fields, "Be who you are! Be who you are! Be who you are!" Can't you see it? One by one, men, women, and children drop cotton sacks and hoes and walk off the fields. Louder and louder they all shout, "Be who you are! Be who you are!" See that free man limping off the farm with the rest of his free brothers and sisters following, their former master yelling at them all the way down the road. You see, there was really no way they could be stopped—they had become free. They just had to start believing in their new identity.

What a great picture of us. We were once completely enslaved to sin with no way out. Through nothing we had done, God in his rich mercy completely pardoned us through Christ's completed work on the cross. Satan might keep shouting, "You're not free. You've always been a slave to sin and you'll always continue to be." But that simply is no longer true. We are free. We have been freed from sin. Start believing in your new identity. Through God's pardon, we no longer have to act like who we were. We can become who we are.

Be Still. Listen to what God is saying to you.

1. Explain how one person, or even several, have influenced you in seeking God's truth.

2. When Paul described how *all* were dead in their trespasses, did your perspective change toward other people, realizing that they are just like you?

3. Say out loud the word *slave* and then stop. Write down the thoughts, emotions, and pictures that come to mind.

4. Maybe there is something in your life God has set you free from, yet you choose to remain entangled in its demands. Describe it. Now pray and ask God to give you strength to walk in his freedom.

Lord, I thank you that today your grace is *comforting* me in these areas:

Lord, I thank you that today your grace is *convicting* me in these areas:

Lord, I thank you that today your grace is *calling* me to:

Today's Memory Verse: Ephesians 2:1

You were dead

"And you were dead in the trespasses and sins in which you once walked, following the course of this world, following the prince of the power of the air, the spirit that is now at work in the sons of disobedience—among whom we all once lived in the passions of our flesh, carrying out the desires of the body and the mind, and were by nature children of wrath, like the rest of mankind. But God, being rich in mercy, because of the great love with which he loved us, even when we were dead in our trespasses, made us alive together with Christ—by grace you have been saved—and raised us up with him and seated us with him in the heavenly places in Christ Jesus, so that in the coming ages he might show the immeasurable riches of his grace in kindness toward us in Christ Jesus. For by grace you have been saved through faith. And this is not your own doing; it is the gift of God, not a result of works, so that no one may boast. For we are his workmanship, created in Christ Jesus for good works, which God prepared beforehand, that we should walk in them."

(Ephesians 2:1-10)

It was the morning of my daughter's third birthday party. We had been praying for good weather because all Grace had asked for was pony rides for all her friends. This automatically meant we had to have an outdoor party! Of the thirty plus family and friends coming over, many were coming to our new home for the first time, therefore, I wanted our yard presentable. I knew this would take a lot of work, and I already had a list of things to do: at the very top was picking up the Barbie cake. Plus, my wife will be the first one to tell you that yard work is definitely not one of my "spiritual gifts."

In a desperate position, I hired a couple of guys to work on the yard. I quickly realized upon their arrival that I had two very competent helpers who knew a lot about hard work, but not a lot about the English language. Nevertheless, I gave them quick instructions, pointing out various places that needed extra work. Looking back, I don't remember all I said, but I do remember pointing to the large patch of monkey grass right by the front porch, telling them to pull out all the weeds. As a matter of fact, because this monkey grass was right by the front porch, I wanted to put extra emphasis on the fact that this part needed to be weeded extremely well. I pointed to the patch and said loudly, "Mucho, mucho pull!" I figured not just "pull," but "mucho, mucho pull" adequately translated that I wanted this place to be weeded with excellence. In response, these two men simply nodded their heads and repeated, "Sí, mucho, mucho." Two hours later when I returned with Barbie cake in hand, these men were still attacking the monkey grass. The problem was that what they understood was very different from what I thought I had communicated. I thought I said to only pull the weeds. They thought I said that I wanted, along with all the weeds, every single blade of monkey grass pulled up from the root. They thought my "mucho, mucho" had meant "don't leave a single growing thing." The guys had done a thorough job, and every living thing was lying on the sidewalk.

Once again, we had a dilemma—a "mucho" dilemma! An hour before the party, with work still undone, the most noticeable spot in the yard looked as bald as an eagle. With so much still to be done, I sent the guys to another part of the yard, letting them know, "Don't worry, I'll fix this."

In a panic, I set the Barbie cake down, daring our puppy to touch it, and began frantically picking up the limp blades and scattering them all over the patch. I thought, *Who will ever know? It only has to look presentable!* With the job completed, it vaguely resembled your granddaddy's comb-over. (If your granddaddy does not have a comb-over, please disregard.) Nevertheless, I didn't care.

I was successful, at least for that afternoon. However, in the next few days, the monkey grass, having been severed at the root, started to turn brown and die. I could stick it back in the soil. I could douse it with water. I could even try to glue each blade back, but the truth was the monkey grass was dead. It might have looked alive that afternoon, but in reality, I had only created a "horticultural comb-over." A mirage.

When the monkey grass was cut off from its source of life, it died. Spiritually speaking, we are no better off than this monkey grass. We are born spiritually severed from our source of life—God. Our sin separates us from God. We can try to make ourselves look presentable, and even fool others with a "spiritual comb-over," but in reality, we're dead in our sins. "For the wages of sin is death" (Romans 6:23).

I could have gone out every day and watered the severed blades. I could have taken spray paint and painted it green again. However, no matter how much I might have attempted to make it appear alive, it was still dead. Parallel that with your life. We can spray-paint our lives, even try to water a dead soul with good deeds; but if it's dead, it's dead. It will not grow.

Paul tells us in Ephesians 2:1 that we were dead. Not drowning, not struggling, not in a spiritual coma, not partially dead, but completely and utterly dead in our sin. If this sounds hopeless, know this is exactly God's intention: hopeless without Christ. In his book *The*

Grace and Truth Paradox, Randy Alcorn states, "You and I, after all, weren't merely sick in our sins; we were dead in our sins. That means I'm not just unworthy of salvation; I'm utterly incapable of earning it. Corpses can't raise themselves from the grave."[1]

If only 99.9 percent of me was dead, then only 99.9 percent of me would need Jesus to come and give me life. If only 99.9 percent of me needed spiritual CPR, then only 99.9 percent of me would be able to give God the glory and credit for my salvation. The reason we need to understand that we are 100 percent dead is so that we can humbly come before God and say 100 percent of us needs 100 percent of him.

Be Still. Listen to what God is saying to you.

1. Think back to a time when you were spiritually dead. Before you became a Christian. How did you spiritually "comb-over" things in your life with the hope of becoming alive?

2. When you realized that 100 percent of you was dead, and that there was nothing you could do on your own to change that, how did you feel about the life Christ gave you by his death?

3. Do you know anyone who is not a Christian? Someone pretending everything is OK (spiritual comb-over) with his soul but lacks a relationship with Jesus?

   How can you extend the grace of God to that person?

4. If you and I are 100 percent dead, and God is 100 percent the giver of life, how much glory do you think God wants for our salvation?

Lord, I thank you that today your grace is *comforting* me in these areas:

Lord, I thank you that today your grace is *convicting* me in these areas:

Lord, I thank you that today your grace is *calling* me to:

Today's Memory Verses: Ephesians 2:1-2

In

*"And you were dead **in** the trespasses and sins in which you once walked, following the prince of the power of the air, the spirit that is now at work in the sons of disobedience—among whom we all once lived in the passions of our flesh, carrying out the desires of the body and the mind, and were by nature children of wrath, like the rest of mankind. But God, being rich in mercy, because of the great love with which he loved us, even when we were dead in our trespasses, made us alive together with Christ—by grace you have been saved—and raised us up with him and seated us with him in the heavenly places in Christ Jesus, so that in the coming ages he might show the immeasurable riches of his grace in kindness toward us in Christ Jesus. For by grace you have been saved through faith. And this is not your own doing; it is the gift of God, not a result of works, so that no one may boast. For we are his workmanship, created in Christ Jesus for good works, which God prepared beforehand, that we should walk in them."*

(Ephesians 2:1-10)

I am a horrible golfer. The few times I have attempted to play, I have ended up spending most of my time in the sand. Ironic: A Middle Eastern guy hanging out in the sand traps. If you put a five iron in my hand (I'm using the lingo, but I really don't know what a five iron is), whether it's a three-hundred-dollar model from the pro shop or a twenty-dollar one from Target, it really won't make a difference. But take that same golf club and put it in Tiger Woods's hands, and immediately it has great value. Such is true with our eternal position.

...dead *in*...

Paul teaches us that we are dead *in* our transgressions and sins. Life is all about whose hands you are *in.* The golf club placed *in* my hand—worthless. The same club placed *in* Tiger's hands—worth a lot. A basketball placed *in* my hands—worthless. A basketball placed *in* Alan Iverson's hands—worth a lot. My life placed *in* the grip of sin—worthless. My life surrendered *in* the hands of God—worthy. As unbelievers, sin owns us—we're *in* it, but that sin also takes up its residence *in* us.

The Bible tells us that we are born *in* sin. We inherited this sinful nature from Adam. It is our disposition, our old self. The Bible teaches us that through Adam, the original man, sin and death entered the world. Romans 5:12 reads, "Therefore... sin came into the world through one man, and death through sin, and so death spread to all men because all sinned." Basically that verse is telling us that we are a part of Adam's lineage and that Adam represents mankind in its sinful nature. To be in Adam (Adamic) is to say that we have inherited his spiritually sinful DNA. That might sound like really bad news, but Romans 5:19 states, "As by the one man's disobedience the many were made sinners, so by the one man's obedience, the many will be made righteous." So just as we are guilty when we are *in* Adam, we are made pardoned when we are *in* Christ. Once again, life is all about *whom you're in.*

In our nature as human beings, we are born sinners. No one has to teach us how to sin. It is our natural tendency. I've never had to sit our daughter Grace down and say to her, "Now today, honey, I am going to teach you how to lie." She, by nature, knows how to crawl into my lap, sporting a purple mustache, and tell me, "No, Daddy, I don't even know where Mommy put the Kool-Aid." We are born that way: sinful and broken. It is our human condition. In Steve McVey's book *Grace Walk,* he explains our condition before we know Christ that "the essence of your existence at that point is that you lived *in Adam.* You were totally dead to God. Since you trusted Christ...you are *in Christ* and your nature is the disposition of Jesus Himself"[1] (emphasis added). We read that we have become "partakers of the divine nature" in 2 Peter 1:4.

One of my favorite commercials featured Taylor Dent, a tennis player who was ranked in the world's top twenty several years ago. He is giving a tennis lesson to a four-year-old boy. Taylor dinks the ball over the net, looking bored. But to his surprise, the boy hits the ball with perfection and power, cramming it down Taylor's throat. By the middle of the commercial, we see Dent and the boy going at it and you get the feeling Dent has met his match on the court. The commercial does a great job of getting your attention. You immediately wonder, *How does a little boy beat a world-class player? Who is this kid?* All of a sudden a minivan drives up, the window rolls down, and the parents blow the horn for the little boy to come get in the van. And then you see it. The boy's parents are Andre Agassi and Steffi Graff, two of the greatest tennis players in history. The commercial is obviously playing off comments that have been made since the day these two tennis pros were married. How many times have they heard people joke, "Wow, think of the amazing tennis players your kids will be!"? Being a tennis buff myself, I had even said, "Can you imagine what their children will be like?" The implication of this commercial is that Andre and Steffi's son can play incredibly well because it's in his blood. It's in his DNA. He can't help it. Think what his parents have passed on to him. In reality, we know this is not completely true. There is no insurance that Andre and Steffi's children are guaranteed to win Wimbledon. But the point is made. It's the boy's inheritance—it's in the genes.

You and I were born with Adam's spiritual genes. Sin is in our blood. It's our inheritance. There is nothing we can do about it. We are broken from birth and desperately in need of salvation. If you're wondering why God set it up this way, author Brennan Manning explains God's intent: "To be alive is to be broken. To be broken is to stand in need of grace."[2] Our hopeless nature highlights our desperation for a savior. It's all about grace.

Be Still. Listen to what God is saying to you.

1. In whose hands are we *in* when we have not received Christ as our Savior?
   In whose hands are we *in* when we have trusted Christ as our Lord and Savior?

2. Spiritually speaking, what did we inherit from Adam?

3. Do my disobedient actions make me a sinner or does my sinful nature make me disobedient? Read this slowly—they might sound a lot alike, but these statements couldn't be more different.

4. Can I do anything to change my Adamic nature on my own?

5. How does the quote by Brennan Manning at the end of today's devotional remind you of who you were before Christ, and who you now are in him?

Lord, I thank you that today your grace is *comforting* me in these areas:

Lord, I thank you that today your grace is *convicting* me in these areas:

Lord, I thank you that today your grace is *calling* me to:

Today's Memory Verses: Ephesians 2:1-2

8 Jonah

Personal ad: Single male, 40. God-centered missionary with no money, looking for like-hearted partner who enjoys walks in the rain and picnics on the beach. Must be committed to preaching the gospel in a faraway land and serving people who will never thank you while living under a government that may persecute you. Blondes preferred.

Notice: At press time my friend "Jonah" is single and available. I have changed his name and identity in order to protect him from harm. He is a missionary in a country where Christian missionaries are not allowed and can be imprisoned if discovered.

Although I constantly tease Jonah, this Asian missionary has become not only a co-laborer in God's work but also a member of our family. Jonah was born in Hong Kong to parents who worked hard to simply make ends meet. Extreme financial pressure caused many problems between his parents, and he was constantly looking for escape. When he was a kid, he struggled with loneliness and depression. Even though his parents were not believers, Jonah and his brother and sisters were allowed to attend a Christian school in Hong Kong. It was there, through the persistent love of a young teacher, that at the age of thirteen he surrendered his heart to Christ. Jonah says he even felt a call to ministry at that point, but never confirmed the call or even told anyone about it. None of his circumstances at home had changed, but he had. He now had hope.

At eighteen years old, Jonah moved to England for four years to continue his education. In many ways he was running from his call to ministry in pursuit of personal wealth and dreams. Sixteen months after he first left home, as he and his brother and sisters were preparing to celebrate the New Year, he received a call that his mother had died of cancer. He didn't even get to say good-bye. This devastated Jonah in many ways but didn't shake his faith. He clung to God even stronger.

Jonah eventually finished his schooling in England and moved to America to be a physical therapist. He again felt God calling him to full-time Christian service. He told me, "By this time, I had everything—a great church, great friends, a great job, and complete financial freedom. I just couldn't find a peace in any of it. I think at the time I knew that God was calling me to be a missionary. I was just scared to let go. I even began bargaining with God, telling him I would go on short-term mission trips and serve him here and there with only brief commitments. But God is not into bargaining."

At the age of thirty-five, Jonah finally surrendered to God's call to be a missionary. He told the Lord that he would go anywhere—except East Asia!! Well, you guessed it. Today, that is exactly where God has him. East Asia.

Often in life, we hand God our brushes and give him instructions on how we want him to paint the canvas of our lives. We know what we want it to look like. Sometimes it's the portrait of comfort, other times the portrait of compromise. But generally, a portrait of grace is neither of the two. When God begins to design our lives as portraits of his grace, his greatest concern is not our comfort, but his glory. By sending Jonah to East Asia, the last place he wanted to go, God created a grace addict. Jonah was willing to walk in the path already set before him. With nothing to depend on but grace, he trusted God more than his own feelings.

Jonah still sometimes struggles with loneliness, and often sees little fruit from his labors, but he knows that God's grace is sufficient. His story is one among the thousands of missionaries that carry out the Great Commission in faraway lands. Like soldiers sent off to fight in the front lines, the mission field is full of casualties. These men and women need more than the church's financial support. They need to know that we are praying for them daily. Do you know any missionaries personally? Have you befriended someone on the field whom you can love and encourage? Again, I'm not asking if your church supports missionaries or if you give to the Lottie Moon offering. I'm asking if you're personally pouring into the life of someone whom God has sent out.

When a missionary receives a box of Cocoa Puffs or a *Sports Illustrated* from a friend, he knows that someone back home cares about how he is doing. Many times the thing that could minister to these brothers and sisters the most is not another copy of *My Utmost for His Highest.* It might just be that they would love a tape of the season finale of *Survivor* simply because they miss watching TV in English. It helps them feel connected to home.

I only wish I could figure out a way to mail Jonah a wife...

Grace Extension

Today's Grace Extension is a call to become a missionary to a missionary. This will involve more than a one-time gesture of grace. As a matter of fact, it is such a rare and unexpected treat for a missionary to have someone reach out to him or her, a continued relationship might even develop. Contact your church denomination's mission board or your local church and ask for a specific missionary's name and address. Write the missionary (or missionary's kid) a letter. Thank them for proclaiming the gospel to the world. Encourage them so they know they are not alone on the journey and that you've got their back. Let them know that if they ever need anything, you will try and get it for them.

Along with the letter, assemble a small package: throw in something practical and fun that they might enjoy receiving. Maybe it's a small packet of Starbucks coffee, maybe a measuring tape with a laser pointer. At the very least, include a magazine like *Sports Illustrated*, *InStyle*, or Martha Stewart's *Prison Living.* As the relationship develops, you will learn their likes and dislikes and will find out birthdays and other important dates. And thanks to e-mails and chat rooms, communication can be more frequent. A part of being called to the Great Commission is to help enable those who have gone before us. As they extend the grace of God to others across the world, you can extend grace to them.

Be Involved!

Today's Memory Verses: Ephesians 2:1-3

Lord, I thank you that today your grace is *comforting* me in these areas:

Lord, I thank you that today your grace is *convicting* me in these areas:

Lord, I thank you that today your grace is *calling* me to:

Today's Memory Verse: Ephesians 2:1-3

Sin

"And you were dead in the ***trespasses and sins in which you once walked,*** *following the prince of the power of the air, the spirit that is now at work in the sons of disobedience—among whom we all once lived in the passions of our flesh, carrying out the desires of the body and the mind, and were by nature children of wrath, like the rest of mankind. But God, being rich in mercy, because of the great love with which he loved us, even when we were dead in our trespasses, made us alive together with Christ—by grace you have been saved—and raised us up with him and seated us with him in the heavenly places in Christ Jesus, so that in the coming ages he might show the immeasurable riches of his grace in kindness toward us in Christ Jesus. For by grace you have been saved through faith. And this is not your own doing; it is the gift of God, not a result of works, so that no one may boast. For we are his workmanship, created in Christ Jesus for good works, which God prepared beforehand, that we should walk in them." (Ephesians 2:1-10)*

My sister is Amish. Well, not really, but she might as well be. In fact, I believe that if Amish people were to come and visit her, they would say, "No, she's definitely not Amish. We're far more liberal and progressive than she is." For years now I have been making this joke, even when she is in the room, and frankly, she loves it. She celebrates her conservatism. Every time I call her a "butter churner," she laughs with delight. When I accuse her of sheltering her children, she replies, "What are you going to accuse me of next—clothing them and feeding them?" To be truthful, I do admire her strong convictions in a day and age when you see parents loading their kids up with sugar and baby-sitting them with an xbox. However, I have to tell you about an incident with her son, Emmanuel.

A few years ago, I stopped at a gas station. Jennifer was driving, with my sister Nastaran in the front passenger seat, and Emmanuel and I were in the back. When I went in to pay for the gas, I picked up a jumbo pack of M&Ms thinking, *Hey, Emmanuel would really enjoy these.* At that time, he was three years old. It doesn't take a rocket scientist to figure out that any three-year-old is going to love some chocolate from his uncle. When I got in the car, Nastaran saw the pack of M&Ms sticking out from my shirt pocket. Deciding to be proactive, she turned to me and said, "You didn't buy that chocolate for Emmanuel, did you? If you did, he is not going to want it. He has decided to be sugar-free." Now let's stop here: no little boy *decides* to be sugar-free. Nastaran then turned to Emmanuel and said, "Now son, tell Uncle David why you have decided to be sugar-free." Emmanuel, with his eyes glued to the package of M&Ms, halfheartedly spouted the verse about his body being a temple for the Lord. My sister then turned to me and said in a bossy tone, "Thou shalt not tempt thy nephew with chocolate. Throwest it away." To which I replied, "Thou art not the boss of me." Needless to say, we got a laugh out of it.

Five minutes later, while Nastaran and Jennifer were deep in conversation, I noticed that Emmanuel was boring a hole in my shirt with his eyes, staring at the M&Ms. While his mom was distracted, I slid the package out of my pocket and quietly whispered, "Psssst, Emmanuel! You want some?" My precious, well-behaved, Bible-quoting, sheltered-as-could-be nephew glanced at his mom to make sure she wasn't looking and nodded his head as if to say, *Whatcha been waiting for?* Within the next ten minutes, he downed the entire pack as I slid them over one by one.

On the last piece, as I was sliding it over, my sister happened to look back and caught me in the act. She abruptly looked over at Emmanuel and said, "Have you been eating chocolate?" Without hesitation, Emmanuel smiled with brown saliva dripping from the corners of his mouth and said, "No, Mommy. I'm sugar-free." We all started to laugh, including my sister.

Even though it seemed like a little "innocent" lie, I was reminded that we are all sinful in our nature. Emmanuel can be sheltered all day, and he can memorize half of the New Testament, but he is still a sinner.

Maybe you're wondering why I'm even calling this a sin. It was just a kid being a kid, right? The truth of the matter is that God's standard is very different than ours. His holy standard is perfection. You and I have categorized sin. We look at the Osama Bin Ladens of the world and say, "Oh, yes, they deserve to fry in hell like a piece of sausage." We look at the little white lies that we tell and little acts of disobedience we commit in our own minds and think, *Surely God's wrath doesn't apply to this.* Well, that simply isn't so. When Paul talks about our sins and transgressions, he is not referring to a certain kind of behavior that makes us dead. In fact, he is talking about every act of sin resulting from our sinful nature. If Emmanuel's only sin his entire life was this M&M sin, it is enough to make him guilty and not measure up to God's standard of perfection.

So what exactly is sin? Is it murder, rape, and adultery? Yes. Is it envy, self-pity, and laziness? Yes. Is it also tempting a little boy to disobey his mom? Yes. Is it also lying to your mom about your disobedience? Absolutely.

Sin is failure, in any way, to obey God's law. This includes not only outward acts of disobedience but even inward thoughts and attitudes. Furthermore, it includes the very being of anyone who does not acknowledge Christ as Savior. Theologian Wayne Grudem makes the statement in his book *Systematic Theology*, "Before we were redeemed by Christ, not only did we do sinful acts and have sinful attitudes, we were also sinners by nature. Even while asleep, an unbeliever, though not committing sinful actions or actively nurturing sinful attitudes, is still a 'sinner' in God's sight; he or she still has a sinful nature that does not conform to God's moral law."[1] In other words, we are condemned not only by our actions, but also by our nature.

This shouldn't be a deep theological revelation, but Christianity 101. Our sinful action is the symptom, and our sinful nature is the disease. It's like having a toothache. The ache is the result of the decay. If I have a decayed tooth that is hurting, I take an aspirin to dull the pain. I have stopped the hurting, but have done nothing to deal with the source of the pain. If I have a sinful nature that makes me sin, I can do all sorts of things to deal with the sin, but I have not really dealt with the source of the problem, which is a sinful nature in desperate need of salvation.

Watchman Nee once said: "Yes, the one who sins is a sinner, but the fact that he sins is merely the evidence that he is already a sinner; it is not the cause. One who sins is a sinner, but it is equally true that one who does not sin, if he is of Adam's race, is a sinner, too, and in need of redemption. Do you follow me? There are bad sinners and good sinners, there are moral sinners and there are corrupt sinners, but they are all alike sinners."[2]

Be Still. Listen to what God is saying to you.

1. What is sin?

2. What are the consequences of sin?

3. Do you ever find yourself categorizing sin?
   Why do you think we do this?

4. As you realize that all of our sins have an eternal consequence, do you find yourself more dependent on Christ and his gift of grace?

5. Write down a prayer of thanksgiving, specifically addressing how he has forgiven your sin and offered you his grace.

Lord, I thank you that today your grace is *comforting* me in these areas:

Lord, I thank you that today your grace is *convicting* me in these areas:

Lord, I thank you that today your grace is *calling* me to:

Today's Memory Verses: Ephesians 2:1-3

Prince and the revolution

*"And you were dead in the trespasses and **sins in which you once walked, following the prince of the power of the air, the spirit that is now at work in the sons of disobedience—among whom we all once lived in the passions of our flesh, carrying out the desires of the body and the mind,** and were by nature children of wrath, like the rest of mankind. But God, being rich in mercy, because of the great love with which he loved us, even when we were dead in our trespasses, made us alive together with Christ—by grace you have been saved—and raised us up with him and seated us with him in the heavenly places in Christ Jesus, so that in the coming ages he might show the immeasurable riches of his grace in kindness toward us in Christ Jesus. For by grace you have been saved through faith. And this is not your own doing; it is the gift of God, not a result of works, so that no one may boast. For we are his workmanship, created in Christ Jesus for good works, which God prepared beforehand, that we should walk in them."*

(Ephesians 2:1-10)

Three comparisons that scripture uses to describe Satan: he is a prince, he is a lion, and he is a liar.

Prince—In Ephesians 2, Paul reminds us that we once walked as dead men, and by following the course of this world; we follow the prince of the power of the air (a fancy way of saying Satan). Satan is the name given to the head of all the demons in the world. Satan is the originator of sin. He sinned before anyone else, including Adam. Satan is a prince who carries out bloody revolutions in our lives. Satan tells us that when we are lost we are his sons of disobedience. The picture he paints of himself is that of a prince, one who has captured us as his sons of disobedience. What we need is a revolution in our lives, one where the Prince of Peace (Jesus) overthrows the prince of the air (Satan).

Lion—The Word of God also calls Satan a lion. As I wrote this devotional, this story came on the news (I kid you not!):

TAIPEI, Taiwan—A man leaped into a lion's den at the Taipei Zoo on Wednesday to try to convert the king of beasts to Christianity, but was bitten in the leg for his efforts. "Jesus will save you!" shouted the 46-year-old man at two African lions lounging under a tree a few meters away. "Come bite me!" he said with both hands raised, television footage showed.

One of the lions, a large male with a shaggy mane, bit the man in his right leg before zoo workers drove it off with water hoses and tranquilizer guns. Newspapers said that the lions had been fed earlier in the day. Otherwise, the man might have been more seriously hurt...or worse. A psychologist said that the man appeared to have psychological issues.[1]

There has been a lot of news lately about people being attacked by lions and tigers. Obviously the most famous incident was Roy of Siegfried and Roy being dragged off stage at the neck by a giant white tiger. Roy had been doing the Las Vegas show for thirteen years, and never had an attack until that night. I'm sure that animal activists say that the lion was probably the "victim." Maybe they blame the fact that Celine Dion singing in Vegas would drive any animal crazy. I don't know, but I'm here to tell you that a giant cat is not to be taken lightly. Personally, I don't particularly care for regular cats and certainly not a giant one with the ability to devour me as an appetizer. Let me just say that lions are not cuddling partners! They have teeth bigger than my left foot! Roy's big mistake in my opinion is that he was trying to *befriend a beast*, which by nature is untamable and violently unpredictable.

Tragically, people today make the same mistake with the devil. They think the devil is not all that powerful and dangerous. Well, the Bible is very clear that the devil is not a furry little kitty that wants to cuddle, but he's a roaring lion who wants to devour and destroy us. In 1 Peter 5:8 we read, "Be sober-minded; be watchful. Your adversary the devil prowls around like a roaring lion, seeking someone to devour." Satan does not want to hurt us or cripple us. He wants to destroy us completely. In the lions' den of spiritual warfare, Satan is in the very thick of this battle. His desire is to sink the claws of legalism and the teeth of sin into us in order to bring about a mortal wound. He is real and so is his plan.

Father of lies—Satan is more than just a lion; he is a lyin' lion!! The Bible says in John 8:44 that Satan is a murderer and a liar. He uses his lies to manipulate people into disobeying God. We are also taught that Satan is deceitful, and we see it throughout scripture from Genesis to Revelation.

John 8:44 calls him the "father of lies." As the father of lies, he has set a course for this world with one thing in mind—destruction. As the father of lies, Satan lies every day. He tells us that the road to happiness and fulfillment is paved with self-indulgence. If we can just satisfy our flesh, we'll be happy. He implies that the guy with the most toys wins; that popularity and fame can make you whole; and that God and conviction get in the way of real joy and pleasure. Tragically, we all too often believe these lies. Just look around and you'll see that the world we live in is not far from the one in which Paul walked.

Outside of being a prince, a lion, and the father of lies, the Bible also calls Satan an enemy, an accuser, a serpent, a murderer, a tempter, an adversary, evil, and a few more things. Paul is reminding us today that when we belonged to Satan, as his servants, we could have labeled ourselves with all of these names. But now the grace of God has given us a new name: "Child of God." Think about this: if in God we have the Holy Spirit, then in Satan we have the unholy spirit. As Christians, "We have not received the spirit of the world but the Spirit who is from God, that we may understand what God has freely given us" (1 Corinthians 2:12 NIV). Thank you Jesus for the revolution of grace. Pray and ask God to give you wisdom as you separate Satan's lies from God's truth. He will also grant you strength to remain firm in your faith despite the circumstances around you.

Be Still. Listen to what God is saying to you.

1. What is the prince of the air's (Satan's) agenda for our lives?

   What is the Prince of Peace's agenda for our lives?

   Think about the revolution that took place in your life when the Prince of Peace destroyed the prince of the air's grip on your life. Write a few sentences of reflection on this.

2. Do you ever see yourself demoting Satan to the significance of a kitty-cat in your life? Much like Siegfried and Roy, do you find yourself playing around with the kitty, just to get attacked by the lion?

3. What are some lies that you have bought into that the father of lies has fed to you?

4. How can you safeguard yourself against Satan, the roaring lion? (Hint: Probably getting in the cage with one is not the best plan, even if you are trying to lead it to Jesus!)

5. In the midst of the battle, how can God's people effectively choose truth over the deceptive lies of Satan?

Lord, I thank you that today your grace is *comforting* me in these areas:

Lord, I thank you that today your grace is *convicting* me in these areas:

Lord, I thank you that today your grace is *calling* me to:

Today's Memory Verses: Ephesians 2:1-3

11 Wrath

"And you were dead in the trespasses and sins in which you once walked, following the prince of the power of the air, the spirit that is now at work in the sons of disobedience—among whom we all once lived in the passions of our flesh, carrying out the desires of the body and the mind, ***and were by nature children of wrath,*** *like the rest of mankind. But God, being rich in mercy, because of the great love with which he loved us, even when we were dead in our trespasses, made us alive together with Christ—by grace you have been saved—and raised us up with him and seated us with him in the heavenly places in Christ Jesus, so that in the coming ages he might show the immeasurable riches of his grace in kindness toward us in Christ Jesus. For by grace you have been saved through faith. And this is not your own doing; it is the gift of God, not a result of works, so that no one may boast. For we are his workmanship, created in Christ Jesus for good works, which God prepared beforehand, that we should walk in them."*

(Ephesians 2:1-10)

Pop..........pop, pop... pop pop pop popopppp...... Don't you just love that sound? For all you hunters out there, no, I'm not talking about gunfire. I'm talking about the sound of popcorn popping. Not just the sound, but also the smell. Not just the smell, but also the taste. It is rare to meet someone who does not love the salty, crunchy taste of popcorn. I'll bet even Dr. Atkins himself snuck off every now and then and had a big, buttery bowl. I remember the first time I let my children help me make a bowl of popcorn for family movie night. Sure, they've eaten plenty of popcorn before, but this time they were getting to be in on the process of making it. At that moment, making the popcorn took precedence over even eating it. We collected the pan, oil, salt, bowl, and corn and I pulled two stools up beside me in front of the stove and turned on the gas flame. "Wow, Daddy, why is that fire blue? It's pretty," remarked Grace as she reached out toward it. In a mad rush I swatted her hand away. Grace looked at me with her hand still stinging, surely thinking, *Why did Daddy just swat me? I only wanted to touch the pretty fire.* I said, "No, Grace, this fire is hot and it will burn you. If you try to touch it again, I will spank you again."

What Grace failed to understand was that the fire could do very different things. On one hand, it is beneficial for cooking popcorn, baking cookies, and making lots of other delicious things. On the other hand, it is fire. It is hot and it is destructive. Yes, it can help produce something delicious to eat; yet it can also destroy with incredible power.

In Ephesians 2:3, Paul reminds us that much like the flame on a stove, our God has many attributes or personality traits. In this passage, Paul reminds us that God is a wrathful God. When he states that we were "objects of wrath" (NIV), he is writing about the wrath of God being rationed out to deserving sinners in a very real place called hell. In his book *Saved from What?* R.C. Sproul reminds us that when you and I are saved, what we are saved from is the wrath of God.[1] Think about it. God saves us from himself. He sacrificed his Son to satisfy his own standard. In other words, it is the grace of God that saves us from the wrath of God. It is love talking when Paul reminds us of this. He is letting us know that only a grace so beautiful could save us from a wrath that is so utterly dreadful. I heard Pastor Alistair Begg once say on his daily radio show, "Wrath made the cross a necessity, but love made the cross a reality."[2]

One might think that it's not love to swat a little girl's hand and ruin her popcorn-making moment, but I disagree. The reason I swatted Grace's hand when she reached for the fire was because I love her. I love her too much not to make her aware of the dangers of fire. Sure, she wants to play with it, but a good father warns his child, telling the truth, even when it comes with a sting. I wanted to prevent Grace from future harm.

Paul spends a lot of time talking about a holy, loving, merciful, good God. God is all of those things. However, Paul would be negligent if he did not also instruct us in God's severity or judgment. In fact, in Paul's letter to the Romans, chapter 11, he states in verse 22, "Consider therefore the kindness and sternness of God" (NIV). If we do not address the fact that we were once objects of the wrath of God, then we can never fully comprehend our pardon from that wrath, nor can we completely appreciate that from which we have been saved. Neither is there any urgency in calling sinners to repentance.

If we love a God who loves all that is righteous and true, then we have to love that same God who hates all that is unrighteous and false. The other side of John 3:16, that God so loved the world that he gave his one and only Son, is the fact that God so hated sin that he acted violently against it. Yes, even toward his beloved Son. Some might believe that a wrathful God is only found in the Old Testament, as if to say that in the New Testament we have a kinder, gentler model. In a rebuttal to that, reread the story of Ananias and Sapphira found in Acts chapter five. Also, in John 3:36 we read, "He who believes in the Son has eternal life; but he who does not obey the Son will not see life, but the wrath of God abides on him" (NASB). Again in Romans 1:18 Paul states, "The wrath of God is revealed from heaven against all ungodliness and unrighteousness of men, who by their unrighteousness suppress the truth." At the end of the day, a god who is at ease about our sin is a god who is not worthy of our worship. A God worthy of praise is a God who sees sin as worthy of judgment. It is this very righteous wrath that condemns you and me, in our unsaved position, to hell.

Jesus used more than a few words in his descriptions of hell. He talked about hell more than anyone else in the Bible. Hell is a real destination, not a state of mind. Jesus described it as a place of utter darkness, where the worms will never die, a place of fire, a place of weeping and gnashing of teeth. Sounds real to me.

In a misguided effort to be loving and graceful, many churches today have walked away from teaching the truth about hell. The misconception is that a hell-less gospel is one that is more appetizing to the lost soul. They are wrong. A hell-less gospel minimizes the power of grace. Without hell, what are we saved from? I know we don't like to talk about it, I know we don't like to sing about it, but as Christians we must not ignore it. To share with a lost world about not only heaven but also hell is to love them with honesty and truth.

When was the last time you heard someone singing about hell? What about God's wrath? Sure, we can sing about his love forever, but we must also recognize his appropriate judgment. Between songs about amazing grace and how his grace is enough, we must also stop and thank him that his grace is enough to satisfy his wrath. So I say, let's keep singing. The next time someone leads a chorus of "Your Love oh Lord," count me in. I will raise my out-of-pitch voice in an attempt to praise God louder than anyone else. But in the middle of the song, let's not lose sight of the fact that just as God's love reaches to the heavens, his wrath reaches the depths of hell. The gore of hell is a backdrop for the glory of heaven; the wrath of God is the backdrop for his grace and mercy.

Be Still. Listen to what God is saying to you.

1. What does the word *wrath* bring to mind?

2. What is God's redemption plan to satisfy his wrath?

3. Why does the church have a tendency to shy away from teaching about God's wrath?

4. How does God's wrath burden your heart for the lost?

5. Write a few sentences about the wrath of God. In some ways you might want this to be a song recognizing God's wrath as appropriate and holy, yet thanking him for delivering you from it.

Lord, I thank you that today your grace is *comforting* me in these areas:

Lord, I thank you that today your grace is *convicting* me in these areas:

Lord, I thank you that today your grace is *calling* me to:

Today's Memory Verses: Ephesians 2:1-3

New Citizenship

When you're a former Muslim from the Middle East who is now doing Christian ministry, you tend to become a magnet for people who are reaching out to their foreign friends. In so many instances, I have found myself at an altar praying with a teenager who is burdened for a Muslim, Buddhist, or Hindu friend who does not have a personal relationship with Jesus Christ. Many times people want to know how they can reach out to someone of a different culture. They always want to know what they can say to connect with people from another part of the world. My answer is always the same: extend grace.

Sometimes, I get to be involved in a different level of the "grace extension." On rare occasions, a student will come forward with a friend who is a new believer in Christ. The friend is introduced as a former Muslim (or person of another religion) who has recently converted to Christianity. In many of these circumstances, the friend wants to know how to deal with parents or family members who will not receive their conversion as good news. My answer is always the same: extend grace.

What separates Christianity from every other religion is that instead of man trying to earn God's favor through good deeds, man receives God's favor through the free gift of grace. To extend God's grace to an exchange student or to your international next-door neighbor is to teach that person the pledge of allegiance. I'm not talking about the American pledge, but our allegiance to the gospel. What the lost soul needs is not to become an American citizen, but to receive citizenship in heaven (Philippians 3:20).

Today, as we look at a group of sophomore girls and how they reached out to a student from Pakistan, we will see a beautiful portrait of grace. Although many e-mails similar to this are received in our office weekly, what makes this one so *real* is that it doesn't imply some fairy-tale ending. The ending is not that the young girl from Pakistan became a Christian and immediately became the most popular girl in the youth group. When this young girl received freedom in Christ, she became a prisoner in her own home. No one can deny that her parents loved her and wanted the best for their daughter. Much like my parents when I became the first Christian in my Muslim home, her parents obviously felt threatened. They viewed their daughter's new belief in Christ as dishonoring and embarrassing. It is important for us all to remember that when God uses us to bring someone home spiritually, that person remains a part of a family that is still ingrained in their culture. Another great thing about this e-mail is that the young girl was not involved in some "behind my parents' back" church-going activity. Both she and the youth ministry maintained integrity and their blameless witness. Here is the e-mail from the youth pastor:

The young girl's name is Mariyam. She is a sophomore in high school whose parents are of the Muslim religion. Recently, some of our youth girls befriended her, and developed a relationship. Through this avenue, the girls and Mariyam began having discussions about their beliefs. Mariyam started to ask a lot of questions and was intrigued. She is a very intelligent girl and is in the top of her class. The girls did their best to explain Christianity to Mariyam. And after some time she made this statement, "I am going to pray to God, and ask him to reveal himself to me through scripture." As soon as the friends heard that, they knew she was close, and that the Lord was working on her. About a week later, Mariyam, in her own room, prayed and asked Christ to come into her life and to save her. We were so excited. However, Mariyam did not want to tell her parents for fear of their reaction. Nevertheless, about a week or so after her conversion, she told her parents, and they could not believe it. She is from Pakistan, and back home she could be killed for what she had done. Her parents tried to force her to reject what God had said. Mariyam's father had been having some health issues, and Mariyam's mother told Mariyam that because of what she had done she was going to give her father a heart attack and be the cause of his death. Her mom, herself, even said she can no longer go on living because of her daughter's actions. Mariyam was forced to tell her who she has been speaking with at school, and that she was not to speak with them anymore. Her mom called the school and even threatened to harm the girls who told Mariyam about Christ. Mariyam is now, besides school, pretty much confined to her home. She cannot leave or spend any time with friends, let alone go with any of them to any church activities. Her parents tried to force Mariyam to throw her Bible away, but after much crying and pleading, they allowed her to keep it. She is allowed to read it only five minutes a day, and then must read twenty minutes from the Koran. They are now thinking about taking her out of the school, but that has not yet happened. I can't imagine all that this girl is going through, but I was finally able to meet her at a football game. She knew who I was through her friends, and when I saw her, she gave me a huge hug. Her face was shining with the light of Christ. She looked at me and said with confidence, "God is with me now, and I know that he is going to help me through all this."

Grace Extension

The Great Commission is, in fact, the ultimate grace extension. We see that so clearly evidenced in today's portrait of grace. These young ladies had a passion not to be stingy with the gospel but to share it with a Muslim friend. No matter where you live, I promise there are people from different cultures intersecting your daily life. Whether it's a neighbor, classmate, or co-worker, most of us know someone who is culturally different, and who may believe that the way to heaven does not involve Jesus Christ. The problem is, in order to earn the right to be heard, we must be willing to go to the trouble of cultivating a relationship with a person of another culture or spiritual belief. Today's Grace Extension is a challenge to build a relationship with someone of a different culture or religion. Think about this: Let's say there is an Asian family who has moved into your neighborhood. Offer to tutor their son after school to help him learn the English language. Take them a "welcome to the neighborhood" gift. Get your church involved. Search the Internet to learn about their homeland and culture. The goal is to extend the grace of God through acts of kindness. Jesus said to go out into the world and preach the gospel...remember that today's Grace Extension goes much further than an assignment in this book. It comes directly from the Word of God.

Another idea for ministering to someone from a different culture: *International Students, Inc.* This foreign exchange student organization will give you and your family the opportunity to sponsor a foreign student who wants to come to the States to study. What an amazing way to do missions without ever leaving home! You can get more information from www.isionline.org.

Be Involved!

Today's Memory Verses: Ephesians 2:1-4

Lord, I thank you that today your grace is *comforting* me in these areas:

Lord, I thank you that today your grace is *convicting* me in these areas:

Lord, I thank you that today your grace is *calling* me to:

Today's Memory Verses: Ephesians 2:1-4

But, wait

"And you were dead
in the trespasses and sins
in which you once walked,
following the prince of the power
of the air, the spirit that is now at
work in the sons of disobedience—
among whom we all once lived in
the passions of our flesh, carrying
out the desires of the body and the
mind, and were by nature children
of wrath, like the rest of mankind.
***But God,** being rich in mercy,*
because of the great love with which
he loved us, even when we were
dead in our trespasses, made us alive
together with Christ—by grace you
have been saved—and raised us up
with him and seated us with him in
the heavenly places in Christ Jesus,
so that in the coming ages he might
show the immeasurable riches of
his grace in kindness toward us in
Christ Jesus. For by grace you have
been saved through faith. And this
is not your own doing; it is the gift
of God, not a result of works, so
that no one may boast. For we are
his workmanship, created in Christ
Jesus for good works, which God
prepared beforehand, that we
should walk in them."
(Ephesians 2:1-10)

When I moved to the U.S. at the age of nine, I learned the English language by watching lots and lots of television. Thanks to the Fonz, Mork, and Scooby Doo, I now make my living proclaiming the gospel via the English language. That might be why, at any given moment in a sermon, I am liable to yell, "Nanoo, nanoo, Ruh-roh," or throw my thumbs in the air and let out, "Ayyyyyyyy."

For some reason in 1979, every day after school there was one commercial shown on television over and over again. It was for the Ginsu kitchen knife. I think today it still holds the record for the longest commercial in TV history. It was the original infomercial. The commercial always started with the plain-old Ginsu knife that could cut, slice, and dice. Then the announcer would excitedly yell out, "But wait, there's more!" and the commercial would continue. The knife would then cut through a shoe, a can, and lots of other things you'd never actually cut with a knife. The announcer then explained how if you bought the Ginsu knife now, you would get a free gift. Just when you thought the commercial was over, he would again yell, "But wait, there's more! Act now and you'll even receive this!" Six or seven "but, waits" later, my young, impressionable mind, which had yet learned how to ask in English where the bathroom was, could flawlessly scream, "But wait, there's more!" (Come to think of it, maybe that's why I got beaten up so often after school!)

In Ephesians 2:4, the apostle Paul gives us the greatest "but wait, there's more" statement in history. This is not a "but wait, there's more" about a bonus gift, but about the gift of grace. In Ephesians 2:1-3 we are confronted with our utter depravity. *Depravity* refers to our inherited moral corruption. We are sinners without hope. To stop at verse three is to walk into the sanctuary that I was referring to in Day 1's devotion and not take the one step to the right. To stop there is to begin to read the story of the woman at the well and put your Bible down before she encounters Jesus. To stop there is to study about a dead man named Lazarus, but to quit reading before Jesus raises him from the dead. It's through these encounters with Jesus that the stories, which all began as tragedies, are turned into testimonies. In John 14:6 Jesus said to his disciples, "I am the way, and the truth, and the life. No one comes to the father except through me." He is the way to take the one step to the right. He is the truth spoken to the woman at the well. He is the life that brought Lazarus forth from the grave.

Allow me to make it personal for a moment: David Nasser was a dead, bankrupt sinner. I followed the ways of the world; doing everything I could to satisfy the cravings of my sinful nature. Because of my disobedience, I was rightfully headed for hell. Romans 6:23 warns, "For the wages of sin is death, but the free gift of God is eternal life in Christ Jesus our Lord."

If my story had ended there, it would have been nothing but tragic. However, when I was eighteen years, two months old, there was a "but, wait" moment in my life. It was on that night that I encountered Jesus, and God forever changed my destiny. I was headed toward severity, but now I walk in his kindness.

Amazing Grace, how sweet the sound
That saved a wretch like me
I once was lost,
But now I'm found
Was blind, but now I see.[1]

Be Still. Listen to what God is saying to you.

1. Who has the ability to change the course of life?

2. Have you ever had a great "but, wait" moment?

3. Do you know someone who needs a "but, wait" moment? Write a specific prayer about that person and ask God how you can be involved.

Lord, I thank you that today your grace is *comforting* me in these areas:

Lord, I thank you that today your grace is *convicting* me in these areas:

Lord, I thank you that today your grace is *calling* me to:

Today's Memory Verses: Ephesians 2:1-4

Mercy

"And you were dead in the trespasses and sins in which you once walked, following the prince of the power of the air, the spirit that is now at work in the sons of disobedience—among whom we all once lived in the passions of our flesh, carrying out the desires of the body and the mind, and were by nature children of wrath, like the rest of mankind. But God, ***being rich in mercy, because of the great love with which he loved us,*** *even when we were dead in our trespasses, made us alive together with Christ—by grace you have been saved—and raised us up with him and seated us with him in the heavenly places in Christ Jesus, so that in the coming ages he might show the immeasurable riches of his grace in kindness toward us in Christ Jesus. For by grace you have been saved through faith. And this is not your own doing; it is the gift of God, not a result of works, so that no one may boast. For we are his workmanship, created in Christ Jesus for good works, which God prepared beforehand, that we should walk in them." (Ephesians 2:1-10)*

There's a Wideness in God's Mercy

There's a wideness in God's mercy
Like the wideness of the sea;
There's a kindness in his justice,
Which is more than liberty.
There's welcome for the sinner,
And more graces for the good;
There's mercy with the savior;
There's healing in his blood.[1]

Whenever you hear of God's mercy, his grace is not far away. In the Bible, God's characteristics of mercy and grace are often linked together. God even describes himself to Moses as, "The LORD, the LORD, a God merciful and gracious, slow to anger, and abounding in steadfast love and faithfulness" (Exodus 34:6). Although these two crucial attributes of God go hand in hand, they are indeed different.

Mercy is God's compassion toward those who suffer. *Grace* is God's compassion toward those who deserve no compassion. Mercy is having compassion for my son who is suffering from a stab wound inflicted by a thief. Grace is having compassion on the thief. Mercy is often deserved. Grace never is. Suppose you're walking down the street and you see a beggar. Your heart breaks for the poor man and you reach for your wallet. Reaching for your wallet shows mercy. Now, suppose as you're pulling your wallet out, the beggar jumps to his feet, punches you in the stomach, and tells you to give him all your money. Grace is taking the money out of your wallet, handing it to the poor man, and then before he runs off, saying to him, "It's cold out here. Why don't you take my coat as well?"

There are people who may argue that a merciful God is not exclusive to Christianity, but none can dispute the fact that a graceful God is. For example, as a former Muslim, I was taught all my life about a God who was merciful. Sure, I had to earn my way toward his love and forgiveness through my good deeds, but I was told that God was merciful because he allowed me to try and earn my salvation. Randy Alcorn tells a story about C. S. Lewis being asked by a room full of scholars what belief, if any, was totally unique to the Christian faith. "That's easy," Lewis replied. "It's grace."[2] Only in Christianity do we see a God who is both merciful and graceful, and fortunately we don't have to choose between God's mercy and grace. We as Christians receive both. Psalm 145:8 tells us, "The LORD is gracious *and* merciful, slow to anger and abounding in steadfast love" (emphasis added).

Stormie Omartian, in her book *Finding Peace for Your Heart*, says "If it weren't for God's grace and mercy, we wouldn't even be saved. For the Bible tells us, 'By grace you have been saved' (Ephesians 2:8) and 'according to his mercy he saved us' (Titus 3:5)."[3] Paul is telling us that God is extending grace to us because he is merciful. God's mercy toward us makes him want to give us his grace. A God of grace and mercy possesses the intense desire to forgive and has the full capability to do so. "The LORD is gracious and merciful, slow to anger and abounding in steadfast love" (Psalm 145:8).

Be Still. Listen to what God is saying to you.

1. The concept of mercy is often thought of as weak. Yet our idea of God is anything but weak. How has God-given mercy directly affected your life?

2. How do grace and mercy differ from one another yet work together in salvation?

3. In a time of extreme pain and suffering, did someone extend a hand of mercy or offer grace to you? Briefly discuss this act of kindness.

4. Psalm 145:8 says, "The LORD is gracious and merciful, slow to anger and abounding in steadfast love." Write about an experience in which you chose to be angry toward someone else, not gracious or merciful. Discuss the person's reaction to your lack of kindness.

   If you had chosen to react with grace and mercy, how would the situation have been improved?

Lord, I thank you that today your grace is *comforting* me in these areas:

Lord, I thank you that today your grace is *convicting* me in these areas:

Lord, I thank you that today your grace is *calling* me to:

Today's Memory Verses: Ephesians 2:1-4

Alive in Christ

"And you were dead in the trespasses and sins in which you once walked, following the prince of the power of the air, the spirit that is now at work in the sons of disobedience—among whom we all once lived in the passions of our flesh, carrying out the desires of the body and the mind, and were by nature children of wrath, like the rest of mankind. But God, being rich in mercy, because of the great love with which he loved us, even when we were dead in our trespasses, ***made us alive together with Christ****—by grace you have been saved—and raised us up with him and seated us with him in the heavenly places in Christ Jesus, so that in the coming ages he might show the immeasurable riches of his grace in kindness toward us in Christ Jesus. For by grace you have been saved through faith. And this is not your own doing; it is the gift of God, not a result of works, so that no one may boast. For we are his workmanship, created in Christ Jesus for good works, which God prepared beforehand, that we should walk in them."*

(Ephesians 2:1-10)

Have you ever wondered about attending your own funeral? I sure have. Who would be there? Would everyone be sad? Would *anyone* be sad? I would love to be able to take a seat and to listen to what people would say about my life. I received a letter a while back from a senior in high school who did just!

Five years ago I was on a conference tour with a ministry called Student Life. I had just published my first book, *A Call to Die.* A few weeks before the end of the tour, I received a letter from a student named Jonathan who had attended the conference tour in Nashville, Tennessee, and had hated every minute of it. He was there only because his friends were there. While his friends ended up surrendering their lives to Christ that weekend, Jonathan continued to care less about the Lord. Afterwards, as a gag gift to his father who was a funeral home director, he bought a copy of *A Call to Die* and threw it in the back seat of his car.

Over the next few days, God used the witness of his friends' new lives to really get his attention and, ultimately, Jonathan received Christ as his Savior. He had forgotten to give *A Call to Die* to his father and decided the devotional could help him in his new walk with the Lord. Throughout the next forty days of struggling through the daily devotions; his classmates, friends, youth-group buddies, and parents all noticed a drastic change in Jonathan. In fact, the change was so huge, that often when his friends would call to talk to Jonathan, his dad would jokingly say, "Jonathan can't come to the phone right now—he's dead!"

After the forty-day journey, Jonathan was excited about having finished the entire book. That Sunday morning before church, he rushed to tell his mom and dad, "Hey, I just finished *A Call to Die.*" Surprisingly, they seemed uninterested. Even at church, his youth pastor and friends acted as if they didn't care either. He became a little discouraged, especially since everyone had been so encouraging.

On the way home from church that afternoon, his father mentioned that he needed to drop by the funeral home to finish up some last-minute things, and asked if everyone in the family would help. Jonathan thought nothing of it. When they entered the sanctuary of the funeral home, much to Jonathan's shock, it was packed with people. These were not just any people, but people from Jonathan's church, family, and school. He wondered who had died. His father asked him to take a seat. After Jonathan sat down, Jonathan's dad stood behind the podium and pointed to the closed casket at the front of the room. He said, "Welcome, everyone, to Jonathan's funeral."

My dad has really lost it this time, thought Jonathan.

One by one the people in Jonathan's life paraded in front of him. Each person talked about not only who Jonathan used to be before Christ but, more importantly, what a different person he had become since coming to Christ. The old Jonathan had died and a new one had been raised up in his place. Jonathan's old nature had been exchanged for Christ's new one.

Jonathan is a perfect example of what Paul is referring to when he says that we are made alive *in Christ.* In Ephesians 2:1-3 he establishes that we were dead in our sins, but here he is letting us know that we are made alive in Christ. If to be dead in sin is destruction, then to be alive in Christ is construction. In 2 Corinthians 5:17 Paul says, "Therefore, if anyone is *in Christ,* he is a new creation. The old has passed away; behold the new has come" (emphasis added). Christ is exchanging the old for the new. To quote Bill Gillham in his book *Lifetime Guarantee*, "The Christian life is not a *changed* life, but an *exchanged* life."[1] It is with the same resurrection power Jesus used to raise Lazarus that he raises us, the dead, and makes us alive. Romans 6:11 states, "So you also must consider yourselves dead to sin and alive to God in Christ Jesus."

Do you see it? When we are in Adam, as we discussed in Day 6, we have an unrighteous nature. It was dead. Once we're in Christ, we exchanged the old nature for a new one (2 Corinthians 5:17). One that is alive. What exactly does it mean to be in Christ? We will find out tomorrow.

Be still. What is the Lord saying to you?

1. In Jonathan's story, we see a noticeable difference in a young man's life; one in which the people around him could not deny Christ's revolutionizing power. Has there been such a dramatic change in your life that people around have noticed?

   List specific ways the Lord has been changing you recently.

2. What was the greatest difference in Jonathan's life? Was it his behavior or his identity? Expand upon this thought.

3. What is the difference between a *changed* life and an *exchanged* life?

4. If we are dead to sin and alive to God in Christ Jesus, then why do we still struggle with sin every day?

Lord, I thank you that today your grace is *comforting* me in these areas:

Lord, I thank you that today your grace is *convicting* me in these areas:

Lord, I thank you that today your grace is *calling* me to:

Today's Memory Verse: Ephesians 2:1

Bobbies

When my little girl, Grace, was just an infant, Jennifer put together a prayer journal for them to pray through every night. (That sounds way more technical and sophisticated than it really was.) In reality, it was a small photo album that contained pictures of people and things to thank God for and to ask his provision for. For example, it included pictures of bread (food), the ocean (God's beautiful world), and relatives (family).

In the back, Jennifer added a couple of pictures of hungry and sick children. Every night Jennifer and Grace prayed for those who were homeless, hungry, sick, poor, and without mommies and daddies. As soon as Grace began to talk, she would ask questions about these children: "Where do they live?" "Why were they crying?" "Why don't they have mommies and daddies?" As she got older, the questions grew tougher: "How can they stop crying?" "Can we send them some food?" "Can they borrow my mommy and daddy?"

One day, Grace decided she had it all figured out. She had recently given up her pacifier, which she affectionately called her "bobby." It was really hard for her, because she loved her bobbies and they always made her feel better whenever she was hungry, hurting, or lonely. Remembering the comfort they brought to her, she asked Jennifer, "Mommy, can we send my bobbies to these children? I think they will make them feel all better."

Grace proceeded to look at all the pictures and decided which child would get which color bobby. The more she talked, the more excited she was.

Capturing that teachable moment, Jennifer got out the bobbies she had hidden in a kitchen drawer, put them in a zip-loc bag with a note, and placed the bag in a padded envelope. She and Grace prayed over the package and then mailed it to an organization we love called Word Made Flesh. Word Made Flesh is a ministry of missionaries living among and ministering to the world's poor, sick, orphaned, and alone. My girls were hoping the missionaries would give these treasures to some street children they encountered. Jennifer knew the chances of a used pacifier ending up in a street child's mouth in India might be slim to none. But her thought was that this would be not only an encouragement to the people opening the envelope but also an exercise in sacrifice for Grace.

Now years later, whenever Grace sees the pictures, she still talks about the bobbies she sent and is certain that God used them to help the children feel "all better." In her mind is a beautiful picture of God's grace. She sees baby girls who are no longer crying because they have pink bobbies in their mouths. She pictures this as she prays for them. And that is a portrait of grace.

Obviously, there are moments in life when we give away things we no longer need. From outgrown clothes, to used appliances, it is great to say, "I cannot use it, but someone else can." Likewise, in the Christian life, to give away something we treasure is to mimic our God. Randy Alcorn's friend Dixie Fraley says, "We're most like God when we're giving."[1]

When God sent us Jesus, he did not give us something he no longer wanted, but he gave a true treasure—his one and only Son. The challenge of giving is to have a loose grip on all our worldly possessions. Sure, Grace's bobbies were used. But to my little girl, her bobbies were everything. By giving away something of great personal value, it made the act very valuable. "For where your treasure is, there your heart will be also" (Matthew 6:21). Through the act of giving, we not only detoxify ourselves from worldly possessions but also intoxicate ourselves with the essence of grace. In fact, sacrificing causes us to be more addicted to grace and less addicted to ourselves. It is the apostle Paul who says it best in 2 Corinthians 8:7: "See that you also excel in this grace of giving" (NIV).

Grace Extension

Today's Grace Extension is short, sweet, and to the point. That doesn't mean, however, that it will be easy. Part of the reason that today's Portrait of Grace was about my daughter is because I'm a dad and have to brag on my kids. But in all seriousness, what I love about my Grace offering her bobbies to a little girl halfway across the world is that those bobbies were very important to her. When Grace decided to share those treasures with the hurting and the poor, she wasn't giving up something she did not care about, but something she held most dear.

Today, I want to challenge you to go to your closet and to find a piece of clothing that you really like. Not something outdated that you never liked in the first place, but maybe something you'd had your eye on for a long time and finally were able to buy. Take it, pray over it, hide a five-dollar bill in one of the pockets, and deliver it to the nearest clothes closet.

If you're not a clothes hog like me, then maybe choose something else that is valuable to you. The idea is to give away something you would love to keep, but would love even more to see someone else receive. Since people from all walks of life are reading this book, I do want to say that if you're a teenager, you need to ask your parents' permission before giving anything away. Remember, extensions of grace always fall under submission to the authority in your life.

Be Involved!

Today's Memory Verses: Ephesians 2:1-5

Lord, I thank you that today your grace is *comforting* me in these areas:

Lord, I thank you that today your grace is *convicting* me in these areas:

Lord, I thank you that today your grace is *calling* me to:

Today's Memory Verses: Ephesians 2:1-5

Parachute

"And you were dead in the trespasses and sins in which you once walked, following the prince of the power of the air, the spirit that is now at work in the sons of disobedience—among whom we all once lived in the passions of our flesh, carrying out the desires of the body and the mind, and were by nature children of wrath, like the rest of mankind. But God, being rich in mercy, because of the great love with which he loved us, even when we were dead in our trespasses, made us alive ***together with Christ****—by grace you have been saved—and raised us up with him and seated us with him in the heavenly places in Christ Jesus, so that in the coming ages he might show the immeasurable riches of his grace in kindness toward us in Christ Jesus. For by grace you have been saved through faith. And this is not your own doing; it is the gift of God, not a result of works, so that no one may boast. For we are his workmanship, created in Christ Jesus for good works, which God prepared beforehand, that we should walk in them." (Ephesians 2:1-10)*

In Ray Comfort's book *Hell's Best Kept Secret*,[1] Ray used an illustration that I want to loosely share with you because it makes a great and very clear point. I believe the story goes something like this...

A man was sitting on an airplane. Unknown to the passengers, a terrorist had hijacked the plane and it was about to crash. Halfway into the trip, the flight attendant carried a parachute over to the man. She asked him to put it on immediately. "Why should I put the parachute on?" asked the man.

"Because it will help make your trip more enjoyable," the flight attendant replied. "Plus, others are putting them on, and you don't want to be the only person without one. Also, you never know what might happen during the flight, and if the plane goes down, it will come in handy."

So the man strapped the parachute tightly to his back, but then he struggled to find a comfortable position in his seat. He saw other passengers who were not wearing their parachutes. They seemed to be enjoying the flight, easily finding comfortable positions in their seats, even taking naps, while the man felt foolish with his on. In fact, some people sat around him pointing and giggling, and the woman sitting directly to his right frowned and firmly pushed his parachute off her side of the seat. Other passengers seemed to only trust the parachutes they could construct themselves, and the gentleman across the aisle frantically tried taping together little drink napkins to create his own.

The man began to think to himself, *The flight attendant lied to me. Not only am I not enjoying this, but there are plenty of people who are not wearing parachutes and they seem to be having a great time. I am sitting here looking like a fool. What are the chances of the flight going down anyway...?*

Picture another scenario: The same man is on the same plane. The same flight attendant walks over to his seat and offers him a parachute. This time however, when he asks the attendant why he should put it on, her answer is very different: "Our flight has just been hijacked by a terrorist. We are about to crash!!!" At that moment the parachute becomes a welcomed piece of equipment. Suddenly, not only does the man not care that the parachute is uncomfortable, he cares even less about how foolish he looks wearing it. He wonders why other passengers are continuing to refuse parachutes, and he frantically tried to convince them to strap theirs on. Comfort takes a back seat to the life-and-death situation on the plane.

Now let's connect the dots. In this illustration, Satan is the terrorist who hijacked the plane, while the flight attendant is anyone who offered the gospel to a lost person. Of course the passenger is you, and the parachute is Christ, our only hope for salvation. Notice that in the first scenario, the flight attendant fails to give the complete, truthful reason why the parachute must be put on. In order to keep the flight "enjoyable," she is withholding a crucial piece of information—the plane is going to crash. Notice the man was shoved by the woman to his right and laughed at by other passengers. This represents the persecution and misunderstandings of our convictions bleeding over into another's personal space. Just as the gentleman across the aisle was taping together the drink napkins, often we try to piece together our good works in a pathetic attempt to build our own salvation, which will do nothing but take us to our certain death.

The purpose of this illustration is to make us understand this truth: without Christ as our salvation, our life is a fatal crash landing. The purpose is not that we put on Christ so that he can make our lives here on earth (the plane ride) easier or more comfortable. In fact, to live in Christ means to look foolish in the eyes of the world. We find in 1 Corinthians 1:18, "For the message of the cross is foolishness to those who are perishing, but to us who are being saved, it is the power of God" (NIV).

In the plane ride of life, to understand that mankind is headed for certain destruction is to put great value on the parachute. Tragically, many people today reject the parachute for a more comfortable ride, distracting themselves with the stale peanuts and B movies of life. It might even be that the flight attendant, with misguided intentions, is keeping the truth of the destruction of the plane a secret in order to allow the passengers to enjoy the rest of the ride. However, as we talked about in Day 11, for the flight attendant to be honest, despite the reaction of the passengers, is for her to be truthful and loving. I pray that we as Christians are not the kind of "flight attendants" who are trying to win a popularity contest on the plane of life.[1]

In all reality, Ephesians 2:1-10, much like Ray's book, is trying to bring honor and glory to the "parachute." Paul does this beautifully by making sure we understand that without Christ we're going to hell. So then when he tells us that together with Christ we are saved, we are ready to embrace the "parachute."

It would be very appropriate at this moment to ask a simple question: Are you together with Christ? Do you have on the parachute of life? Is Jesus Christ your Lord and your Savior? If, under the conviction of the Holy Spirit, you sense him calling you from eternal death to eternal life, then I say come and embrace Jesus the Savior. Acknowledge that you're a sinner and that there's nothing you can do on your own to save yourself. Recognize that Jesus Christ, the Son of God, lived the perfect life on earth, yet willingly died a sinner's death on the cross. It was on that cross he paid the debt for our sin. Abandon all you've done—not just the bad stuff, but even your self-righteous good acts. Bring all of it completely before Jesus and ask for forgiveness and peace. He will change your nature—not just your behavior, but also your identity.

"I have been crucified with Christ. It is no longer I who live, but Christ who lives in me. And the life I now live in the flesh I live by faith in the Son of God, who loved me and gave himself for me" (Galatians 2:20).

Be Still. Listen to what God is saying to you.

1. In Ephesians 2, Paul says that when we are together with Christ we are made alive. Who is the one who makes us alive?

2. Spiritually speaking, who is the "flight attendant" in your life?

3. In the airplane illustration, the flight attendant appeared to be a nuisance when asking the passenger to put on the parachute. Have you ever felt like a nuisance when you witnessed to a friend? Explain.

4. What is the passenger trying to piece together little drink napkins to make his own parachute referring to?

5. Again, in the airplane illustration, we are reminded as Christians that we are not putting on the "parachute" for comfort's sake, but for eternal security. Do you ever lose focus of that? Write about a time when you felt inconvenienced and uncomfortable because everyone else on the plane ride of life thought you were foolish for wearing the "parachute."

Lord, I thank you that today your grace is *comforting* me in these areas:

Lord, I thank you that today your grace is *convicting* me in these areas:

Lord, I thank you that today your grace is *calling* me to:

Today's Memory Verses: Ephesians 2:1-5

The wondrous cross

*"And you were dead in the trespasses and sins in which you once walked, following the prince of the power of the air, the spirit that is now at work in the sons of disobedience—among whom we all once lived in the passions of our flesh, carrying out the desires of the body and the mind, and were by nature children of wrath, like the rest of mankind. But God, being rich in mercy, because of the great love with which he loved us, even when we were dead in our trespasses, made us alive together with **Christ**—by grace you have been saved—and raised us up with him and seated us with him in the heavenly places in Christ Jesus, so that in the coming ages he might show the immeasurable riches of his grace in kindness toward us in Christ Jesus. For by grace you have been saved through faith. And this is not your own doing; it is the gift of God, not a result of works, so that no one may boast. For we are his workmanship, created in Christ Jesus for good works, which God prepared beforehand, that we should walk in them."*
(Ephesians 2:1-10)

Freedom fries. Since the beginning of Operation Iraqi Freedom, when America went to war with Iraq and the French denounced it, Americans everywhere launched a campaign of patriotic revolt. No, we did not stop all tourist flights to France or put them in a trade embargo. We did something much more severe. We took out our Sharpies® and attacked menus all over the country. French fries became "freedom fries"; french vanilla became "freedom vanilla"; and even french toast became "freedom toast."

However, my family and I did not have that luxury. My father owns a restaurant named "Café de France," and it would have almost been impossible to rename it "Café de Freedom"! As a family, even though we might not be the biggest fans of France's political agenda, we grew up loving the city of Paris. I can honestly say that I've been there more times than I can count. What draws us to Paris is the art, the food, and the romance (definitely not the politics). Just about every time we go to Paris, we make sure we visit the world's greatest art museum—The Louvre. I think the word *Louvre* is French for "long lines"! The long lines are well worth the wait, though. Holding some of the world's greatest masterpieces, the Louvre is home to millions of pieces of art, including the most famous painting in all of history, Leonardo da Vinci's *Mona Lisa.*

In the first year that Jennifer and I were married,

my father took our entire family to France. There were seven of us altogether, including my little brother Benjamin. If you've ever heard me speak, I'm sure you already know about Benjamin. I can't say enough about him. But just in case you don't know him, let me say that Benjamin is an extraordinary young man. Having Down's syndrome causes Benjamin to be simple and real. Benjamin doesn't know how to play the games in life that so many of us have gotten so good at playing. As with most Down's syndrome children, he wears his emotions on his sleeve. If he loves you, he doesn't let go; if he is mad at you, he doesn't hold back; if he's crying, he doesn't care if he's in public. I've yet to meet anyone who loves Jesus like Benjamin does. Never was that more clear than when we took Benjamin to The Louvre. I told a much shorter version of this story in *A Call to Die*, but it's so great I'm compelled to tell it again.

It was a cold morning, and as we entered The Louvre, Jennifer and I were assigned to look after Benjamin. The problem was that we didn't have all day, and our mission was to see the *Mona Lisa.* As Jennifer opened the big map and we began navigating room to room, we got so caught up in looking for the *Mona Lisa* that we realized we hadn't seen Benjamin in twenty minutes. We were panicked! We had lost my very special brother in one of the largest castles on the planet! We started to backtrack, yelling his name from room to room. We even asked for help from the French security guards. Suddenly, I heard out of one of the guards' walkie-talkies, "La Croix, La Croix!" followed by a bunch of words I didn't understand. The guard took off with us not far behind. As we entered a room, we found Benjamin sitting in a chair in front of the largest painting of the cross I had ever seen in my life. He was weeping uncontrollably.

As I walked in, I remembered that room—we had all walked through it, using it as a shortcut in our search for the *Mona Lisa.* I remember walking quickly by the painting and thinking, *Wow! That's one huge painting of the cross.* But to Benjamin, it was more than a shortcut to the *Mona Lisa.* It was something he couldn't just walk by and glance at. He had to stop at the foot of the cross. I saw how the cross affected him: He simply could not just walk by.

My prayer is that, today, the cross will stop us in our tracks. By the way, let me just say that there was no chair sitting under the cross painting that day. Benjamin had somehow found a chair (who knows where) and made himself a place to survey the cross. I hope we will all do the same.

Tomorrow, we will look at the classic acronym for **GRACE**—**G**od's **R**iches **At** **C**hrist's **E**xpense. It would serve us well to not rush by Christ's *expense* to get to God's *riches.*

Be still. Listen to what God is saying to you.

Michael Card's book *A Violent Grace*[1] was a vehicle God used in my life a few years ago to help me really reflect on the cross. Today, instead of using discussion questions as a tool for meditation and reflection, use the titles of the twenty-one chapters in Michael's book. Rather than answering questions, stop and think about Jesus. This is not a "sit back and grab a cup of coffee" kind of moment. Instead, find a place where you can get into a posture of humility, and one by one slowly ponder the next twenty-one statements.

1. He was born to die so I could be born to new life.
2. He suffered temptation so I can experience victory.
3. He was betrayed so I might know his faithfulness.
4. He was arrested and bound so I could be rescued from bondage.

Stop. Take a few moments and meditate on these first four truths about Jesus Christ.

5. He stood trial alone so I might have an advocate.
6. He was wounded so I could be healed.
7. He endured mockery so I could know dignity and joy.
8. He was condemned so the truth could set me free.

Again, stop. Take your time and reread the last four statements, thinking about what Christ did for you.

9. He was crowned with thorns so I might crown him with praise.
10. He was nailed to the cross so I might escape judgment.
11. He was stretched out between thieves so I could know the reach of love.
12. He suffered thirst so I could drink living water.

Go back again and think upon Jesus and all that he did upon the cross. Drink slowly.

13. He said, "It is finished," so I could begin my walk of faith.
14. He was God's lamb, slain so I could claim his sacrifice as my own.
15. He was forsaken by the Father so I would never be rejected.
16. He chose the shame of weakness so I can know the hope of glory.

Pray a prayer of thanksgiving to the Lamb of God who showed his strength by choosing weakness.

17. He shed his blood so I can be white as snow.
18. His heart was pierced so mine could be whole.
19. He died and was buried so the grave could not hold me.
20. He rose again so I might experience eternal life.

Take a moment and meditate in celebration that indeed the tomb is empty.

21. He is known by his scars so I will take up my cross and follow Him.

    If you have time, go back and read these truths again.

"He was despised and rejected by men; a man of sorrows, and acquainted with grief; and as one from whom men hide their faces he was despised, and we esteemed him not. Surely he has borne our griefs and carried our sorrows; yet we esteemed him stricken, smitten by God, and afflicted. But he was wounded for our transgressions; he was crushed for our iniquities; upon him was the chastisement that brought us peace, and with his stripes we are healed" (Isaiah 53:3-5).

Sing with me...

When I survey the wondrous cross,
On which the Prince of glory died,
My richest gain I count but loss,
And pour contempt on all my pride.[2]

Lord, I thank you that today your grace is *comforting* me in these areas:

Lord, I thank you that today your grace is *convicting* me in these areas:

Lord, I thank you that today your grace is *calling* me to:

Today's Memory Verses: Ephesians 2:1-5

God's riches at Christ's expense

*"And you were dead in the trespasses and sins in which you once walked, following the prince of the power of the air, the spirit that is now at work in the sons of disobedience—among whom we all once lived in the passions of our flesh, carrying out the desires of the body and the mind, and were by nature children of wrath, like the rest of mankind. But God, being rich in mercy, because of the great love with which he loved us, even when we were dead in our trespasses, made us alive together with Christ—**by grace you have been saved**—and raised us up with him and seated us with him in the heavenly places in Christ Jesus, so that in the coming ages he might show the immeasurable riches of his grace in kindness toward us in Christ Jesus. For by grace you have been saved through faith. And this is not your own doing; it is the gift of God, not a result of works, so that no one may boast. For we are his workmanship, created in Christ Jesus for good works, which God prepared beforehand, that we should walk in them."*

(Ephesians 2:1-10)

I'm not a gambling man. But if I were, I would put money on this: if you grew up in the church, you probably have written in your Bible somewhere the famous GRACE acronym:

G—**G**od's
R—**R**iches
A—**A**t
C—**C**hrist's
E—**E**xpense

You may have even received a pixie stick at VBS for memorizing it. There is good reason that this elementary acronym has been able to stand the test of time. In its simplicity, there is great truth. However, the actual grace of God is anything but simple. If it doesn't completely blow your mind, you don't get it. That's why we call it "Amazing Grace." Let's look at this unmerited favor.

In the courtroom of life, you and I are guilty of a sinful nature. Our guilt condemns us to the death penalty. This is due justice. It is only fair that since we are guilty of sin, we be condemned. God, on the other hand, is a perfect and holy God who is sinless and right. He hates the sin, yet he loves the sinner. However, as a God who is fully just, while he loves us, this doesn't mean he can simply overlook our sin. In order for justice to be carried out, the penalty for our sin must be paid. The problem is we don't have what it takes to pay it. We can't be good enough, go to church enough, or write a tithe check big enough to earn his forgiveness. So, **G**od who is **R**ich in mercy **A**llowed **C**hrist to pay the **E**xpense. When we accept Christ as the only one who can pay the debt for our sins, we receive forgiveness. We don't deserve forgiveness—Jesus didn't deserve death. If this sounds unfair, it's because it is. God's grace is not fair—it's so much better. It's so much bigger. By the way, this was God's plan, not man's plan. Through grace, God maintains his justice while at the same time showing forgiveness. Through grace, in the eternal scope of things, not only does God set the standard, but he also fulfills it. The standard setter himself becomes the sacrifice. What a God-sized idea! Man could never have thought of such an outrageous plan of redemption. What scandalous grace! We find forgiveness and pardon because Christ served the sentence for us. But it doesn't just stop there. He not only forgives us, but he also takes us in. As his children, even when we continually fail, he continues to forgive time after time. Grace never stops.

London is home to some of the most beautiful churches in the world, such as St. Paul's Cathedral, Westminster Abbey, and even the former church of Charles Spurgeon. However, on the second night of our honeymoon Jennifer and I slipped into a packed room to attend, what we still call today, one of the greatest worship experiences ever. Our worship experience wasn't in one of these great churches; it was in the west end of town, right in the middle of the theatre district. We were at the musical *Les Miserables*, adapted from Victor Hugo's great novel.

Les Miserables is the story of a man, Jean Valjean, who steals a loaf of bread to feed his starving nephew. When caught by the law, he is sentenced to life in prison. He eventually escapes from prison and finds refuge in the home of a godly bishop who gives him shelter. Instead of being thankful for the man's generosity, Jean Valjean steals a silver candlestick and tries to escape in the middle of the night. In the midst of escaping from the bishop's house, an officer of the law catches Valjean with the candlestick in his hand. The officer wakes the bishop up and says, "The man that you have sheltered has stolen from you. Is this not your candlestick?"

In a merciful act of generosity, the bishop replies, "Yes, this was my candlestick, but now it is his. I have given it to him." The bishop then looks at Jean Valjean and says, "Look, friend, you only took with you one candlestick. You must take the other that completes the set." The bishop then gives Valjean the other candlestick as an act of scandalous grace. Grace never stops. This radical act forever altered the course of Jean Valjean's life. He becomes a portrait of grace. In the rest of the play, we see Valjean display grace over and over again to others. We see a man living the grace-filled life. It's important to point out that Jean Valjean did not think to himself, *Hey, this bishop guy undeservingly gave me all his silver! This makes me want to go and take advantage of him even more. I'm going to go to his house tonight and rob it. The bishop is apparently passive, and not into pressing charges.* No, the exact opposite happens. The graciousness of the bishop proves not to be passive, but powerful and life altering for Jean Valjean.

In the courtroom of life, we are guilty of stealing the "silver." However, God not only forgives us but says, "I'm going to bless you as well." Many in the church are afraid of a God like that. They think that a God as grace-full as the bishop in *Les Miserables* will be passive. The fear is that a grace message this radical will give people license to sin. Some may say, "This kind of redemption will encourage people to go back and steal even more silver." Sadly, I used to think the same. But now I know better. No, the exact opposite happens. Just like Jean Valjean in the play, God's amazing grace sets us on a path of grace-driven purpose. Grace doesn't give us license to sin. It gives us the motivation and ability to stop sinning.

Within the first twenty minutes of this play, we see a man condemned to life imprisonment because he has broken the law. He is a thief. But more importantly, we see a bishop who personifies the grace of God.

What a beautiful picture of grace! God not only withholds from us what we deserve, but he also gives to us what we can never deserve. Charles Wesley said it best when he penned the words in his hymn "O for a Thousand Tongues to Sing":

> *He breaks the pow'r of cancelled sin,*
> *He sets the pris'ner free,*
> *His blood can make the foulest clean,*
> *His blood availed for me.*[1]

Be still. Listen to what God is saying to you.

1. In the courtroom of life, what are we guilty of?

   What are we condemned to?

2. Why can't God just let bygones be bygones when it comes to our sinful nature?

3. What role does grace play in the courtroom of life?

4. In the musical *Les Miserables*, what does the silver represent?

   Has there ever been a silver moment in your life? Discuss in detail.

5. Rewrite Wesley's "O for a Thousand Tongues to Sing," adding your name in all four lines. After rewriting it, slowly meditate on each sentence before you begin to journal.

Lord, I thank you that today your grace is *comforting* me in these areas:

Lord, I thank you that today your grace is *convicting* me in these areas:

Lord, I thank you that today your grace is *calling* me to:

Today's Memory Verses: Ephesians 2:1-5

Portrait of Grace

Pardoned

Grace, grace, God's grace
Grace that will pardon and cleanse within;
Grace, grace, God's grace
Grace that is greater than all our sin.[1]

"Guilty as charged!" The gavel echoed through the courtroom as Dan sat stunned, thinking, *How in the world did I end up here?*

Dan Moran grew up in church. In the Deep South, the question isn't so much, "Do you go to church?" but "Where do you go to church?" This small-town Alabama athlete grew up in a Christian home with Dad involved in church leadership and Mom baking goodies for Vacation Bible School. He became a Christian at age seventeen. How many times have we all seen a seventeen-year-old give his life to Christ at a Christian event, only to wonder about the rest of his life? For Dan, everything looked promising. A year later on a mission trip, Dan knew God was calling him to ministry. "I wanted to make a lot of money in life. I also wanted to be cool. Being a minister didn't seem to be able to help me achieve either. So I ran away. Not just from my call to ministry, but even from being obedient to God in everyday life." And so this began his prodigal years.

By the time he was twenty-three years old, Dan was climbing the corporate ladder, making money and creating a reputation for himself. One cold and rainy night in November, Dan left an awards ceremony after having just received the top award in marketing. He made his way into a bar to celebrate by having a few drinks, and then found himself a few hours later in a car accident that took the lives of an elderly couple. Two months later, a deputy sheriff arrested Dan and he was charged with two counts of manslaughter in the first degree. Dan says, "I knew a lot of influential people and I figured I could get out of this. But on the day of judgment, I was convicted on both counts. I should have been. I was guilty. A few months later on the day of sentencing, I piled forty plus people into the courtroom to speak to the judge on my behalf. One by one these people took the stand and talked about what a great guy I was. By the time the last person stepped down, I thought I was home free."

Then the judge asked one final question: "Is there anyone else who has something to say before I give my sentence?" At that moment, the daughter of the elderly couple stood up and said two simple sentences: "I am not a vindictive person, but I wish justice to be served here today. That was my mom, my dad, and my children's grandma and grandpa that boy killed with his car." Then she sat down.

With the power of one testimony, the forty before it seemed to fade away. The judge sentenced Dan to two three-year terms in prison. What seemed like a life of promise and prosperity had turned into one of disaster.

One night, as Dan was sitting in his cell, he got the news that took this tragedy and turned it into testimony. The same judge who had sentenced Dan to prison had, as an act of scandalous grace, pardoned him. Although Dan confesses today that he deserved so much more than even the sentence he got, it was that act of unmerited favor that began to turn his life around.

Eventually, ten years after his initial call, Dan surrendered to full-time ministry. Today, Dan, his wife Debbie, and their son Seth, have served in over thirty-nine states and eleven countries proclaiming the pardoning power of the gospel. This grace addict recognizes what it truly means to be pardoned. Not only in the physical sense but, more importantly, in the eternal sense. In Dan Moran's life, the law was not at fault; Dan was. The law painted a portrait of due punishment, but grace painted a portrait of unmerited pardon and forgiveness.

Grace Extension

Most of us don't know anyone serving time in prison. We daily take for granted the freedom and comfort that we have. Today's Grace Extension will be a call to connect with a prisoner. The intent behind this Grace Extension is to be an influence and encouragement to someone who is without their physical freedom.

Let me give you two options:

Option #1: You can connect with a prisoner or his/her family through Prison Fellowship ministries. This is an organization founded by Chuck Colson that specifically focuses on ministering to those behind bars. Logging onto www.PFM.org will show you the different ways you can become involved in witnessing to and encouraging prisoners all over the

United States. Rightfully so, many people today are afraid to reach out to prisoners due to safety issues. Chuck Colson has found ways for this kind of ministry to happen with no risk. There are literally dozens of ways for you to affect the lives of prisoners, from helping with a Christmas list for prisoner's children, to writing an encouragement card. What a difference God can make through you!

Option # 2: The second way you could extend grace would be to reach out to a Christian brother or sister who is in chains for their faith. Many governments all over the world imprison, torture, and kill Christians because of their loyalty to Jesus Christ. Voice of the Martyrs is an organization dedicated to helping these persecuted believers. Log onto www.persecution.com to explore all the opportunities Voice of the Martyrs has available for ministry. From writing a letter to a brother or sister in Christ who is in prison halfway across the world, to petitioning a government official and asking for the release of an inmate, I'm sure you will find something that stirs your heart. This organization has thought of everything—right down to providing sample letters. I encourage you to check out this website even if you do not choose this particular grace extension. If nothing else, it will broaden your concept of Christianity and hopefully encourage you to at least pray for the persecuted church.

I think it is crucial to remember that when we minister to someone in desperate circumstances, like one in prison, we are serving Christ himself. Christ tells us in Matthew 25, "For I was hungry and you gave me food...I was a stranger and you welcomed me, I was naked and you clothed me, I was sick and you visited me, I was in prison and you came to me...Truly I say to you, as you did it to one of the least of these my brothers, you did it to me." What a great motivating factor.

Be Involved!

Today's Memory Verses: Ephesians 2:1-6

Lord, I thank you that today your grace is *comforting* me in these areas:

Lord, I thank you that today your grace is *convicting* me in these areas:

Lord, I thank you that today your grace is *calling* me to:

Today's Memory Verses: Ephesians 2:1-6

Oprahnym

"And you were dead in the trespasses and sins in which you once walked, following the course of this world, following the prince of the power of the air, the spirit that is now at work in the sons of disobedience—among whom we all once lived in the passions of our flesh, carrying out the desires of the body and the mind, and were by nature children of wrath, like the rest of mankind. But God, being rich in mercy, because of the great love with which he loved us, even when we were dead in our trespasses, made us alive together with Christ—by grace you have been saved—and raised us up with him and seated us with him in the heavenly places in Christ Jesus, so that in the coming ages he might show the immeasurable riches of his grace in kindness toward us in Christ Jesus. For by grace you have been saved through faith. And this is not your own doing; it is the gift of God, not a result of works, so that no one may boast. For we are his workmanship, created in Christ Jesus for good works, which God prepared beforehand, that we should walk in them."

(Ephesians 2:1-10)

Oprah. There's only one. Certainly there are other Oprahs out there, but when I say the name "Oprah," only one person comes to mind. On her season premiere, September 13, 2004, daytime television's diva made headlines all over the world. She gave away 276 brand-new, loaded Pontiac G6 cars, *in one show!* The talk around the water cooler everywhere the next morning was about Oprah's unusual generosity.

A couple from my hometown of Birmingham was in the audience that day as Oprah decided to have the biggest car giveaway of all time. A few days later I heard the woman on a local radio talk show. She and her husband had gotten tickets to the Oprah show as a birthday gift. They arrived, having no idea what the show would be about, and watched as a car was driven onto the stage. The audience was told that under every seat there was a box, and the lucky audience member who had a key in the box would win the car. At the right time, the audience was asked to place the boxes from under their seats on their laps, then instructed, "Open the boxes and let's see who has won a car." Imagine everyone's amazement when every single box contained a key! Yes, the lady and her husband each won a car of their own.

Having said all that, I remember the lady thanking God on the radio for such a timely and unexpected gift. She understood that the car did not ultimately come from Oprah, but Pontiac, who had provided them to Oprah. The lady also understood that Pontiac relied on many people with God-given intelligence created and produced these automobiles. Furthermore, these people were able to produce the car from resources and parts that were provided from factories, who in turn processed them from things in the environment. Ultimately, the Creator creates every single thing in the environment. Therefore, when the lady thanked God for her new car, she was appropriate in doing so.

There are two different manifestations of God's grace: common and saving. We will focus right now on God's common grace. Common grace is the grace of God given to *all* people, not as a part of salvation, but as an act of kindness toward this world. It's God's common grace that explains why saved and unsaved people can have air to breathe, water to drink, food to eat, and cars to win on the Oprah show.

Getting back to the Oprah show, I want to use that day's episode to discuss a few principles concerning the common grace of God. I will attempt to explain it with an "Oprahnym." (No, not Acronym – Oprahnym!)

O – One does not have to be saved to receive God's common grace. When it rains on my front lawn, it also rains on my neighbor's lawn. God does not say, "David's neighbor is not a Christian and because he has not received my saving grace, he will not receive any rain today." God is the giver of the rain, but the rain is common to all people. He is the creator of automobiles, but that day at the Oprah show, he did not allow only Christians in the audience to win them.

P – People are not saved by common grace. Common grace does not result in salvation. Common grace can *lead* to saving grace, but only saving grace results in salvation. That day, just because Oprah had the financial means (through common grace) to have a bunch of cars to give away, that is not an indication that she is going to heaven. In simpler terms, you can be very rich here on earth due to the blessings of common grace, but until you accept saving grace, you will be eternally bankrupt.

R – Reaping the benefits of common grace should bring us to a place of worship and adoration. When we realize that all good things come from God, and we see the creative ways that he has allowed us to enjoy our lives, it blows our minds. God, in common grace, not only gives us food to eat but gives us the taste buds to savor the bread as well as the sweet taste of strawberries. Through common grace he gives us new depth to the word *red* with a perfectly ripened tomato and to the word *blue* with a cloudless summer sky. All of these things, every grain of sand to every mountaintop, proclaim the grandeur of our God and should cause us to worship him. It is common grace that allows the woman who won the car to stir her heart to thanksgiving toward someone much bigger than Oprah.

A – All good things come from God. Every invention—everything good, from indoor plumbing to refrigeration, is a gift of common grace. In common grace, God does not limit the invention or advancement of science and industry by only using Christian scientists and inventors. That day at the Oprah show, a Christian would not have to say, "I can take the body of the car, but I cannot accept the tires or the windows, because tires and windows were invented by nonbelievers." He or she could accept and appreciate the whole car.

H – Having a charitable heart can be evidence of common grace in the life of even non-believers. From Bill Gates to Lance Armstrong, we see people every day who do not claim to be followers of Christ, yet they show great acts of kindness and charity to others. Although lost people do not know or understand this, every act of good is rooted in God's common grace. That afternoon Oprah might have given the cars away to celebrate the anniversary of *her* show, but ultimately God deserves the glory.

Now, we're done with Oprah, on to Dr. Phil...

Be still. Listen to what God is saying to you.

1. What is God's common grace, and how does it differ from God's saving grace?

2. Do the words *common* and *grace* used together seem to contradict each other? Is it a bit of an oxymoron (kind of like the words *jumbo shrimp*)?

3. How do you and I, as Christians, benefit from God's common grace to unbelievers—such as scientists, inventors, doctors, etc.?

4. Be honest. Do you ever struggle with a nonbeliever receiving God's common grace in a particular way, when you, as a believer, didn't receive it? (Example: A girl at school who is a nonbeliever drives a very nice car, and you, as a believer, ride your bike to school.) Even the psalmist David struggled with this. Read Psalm 73.

5. How can God's common grace be used as a tool for evangelism? Be specific. Writing with a particular person in mind, come up with a game plan for sharing Christ with that person, utilizing the thought that they've been blessed by God's common grace already.

Lord, I thank you that today your grace is *comforting* me in these areas:

Lord, I thank you that today your grace is *convicting* me in these areas:

Lord, I thank you that today your grace is *calling* me to:

Today's Memory Verses: Ephesians 2:1-6

Grace addict

*"And you were dead in the trespasses and sins in which you once walked, following the prince of the power of the air, the spirit that is now at work in the sons of disobedience— among whom we all once lived in the passions of our flesh, carrying out the desires of the body and the mind, and were by nature children of wrath, like the rest of mankind. But God, being rich in mercy, because of the great love with which he loved us, even when we were dead in our trespasses, made us alive together with Christ—**by grace** you have been saved—and raised us up with him and seated us with him in the heavenly places in Christ Jesus, so that in the coming ages he might show the immeasurable riches of his grace in kindness toward us in Christ Jesus. For by grace you have been saved through faith. And this is not your own doing; it is the gift of God, not a result of works, so that no one may boast. For we are his workmanship, created in Christ Jesus for good works, which God prepared beforehand, that we should walk in them."*
(Ephesians 2:1-10)

Stop breathing. Seriously, stop. Let's begin today's devotion with this mental exercise. I want you to concentrate hard, hold your breath, and have your mind tell your lungs to quit pulling in oxygen for the next seventy-seven minutes. Remember, this is an exercise of the mind—no external help. Ready, set, go! Couldn't do it, could ya? Of course not!! You've just proven to yourself that you're an air addict! No matter how hard you try to command your lungs to stop breathing, they simply won't stop. Your lungs are utterly dependent upon air to survive. So much so, that your lungs have signed an exclusive, lifetime contract with oxygen. Air is the only thing they want to breathe, and they can't get enough of it.

The word *addict* is defined as the following: to cause (someone or oneself) to become dependent on something.

Our souls are our spiritual lungs. Just as our lungs need constant air, our souls need constant grace. If our lungs are air addicts, then our souls are grace addicts. As a true air addict, I must believe that I cannot survive without my addiction to air being satisfied. I must believe that *only air* can satisfy my lungs. Nothing else will do. In other words, unless I breathe air, I cannot survive. The same is true about being a grace addict. In order to be a true grace addict, I must believe that my soul cannot survive without my addiction to grace being satisfied. I must believe that *only God's grace* can satisfy my soul. Nothing else will do. In other words, unless I have God's grace, my soul cannot survive.

As long as there is an endless supply of air to breathe, I am a satisfied air addict. Spiritually speaking, as long as there is an endless supply of grace (which there is), I am a satisfied grace addict.

Now slide over to a different rail of thought, a rail that runs side by side with the rail of truth about our grace addiction. In your mind, imagine these two rails of thought running parallel to form a track—much like a railroad track. These two ideas don't contradict one another. Instead, they run side by side, complimenting each other. Rail 1: One can't get enough of God's grace. Rail 2: God's grace is more than enough to satisfy needs in every circumstance. In other words, his grace is sufficient. If these two rails are aligned, you will be on the track that leads to a victorious life.

The sufficiency of grace means that the endless supply of God's grace can satisfy every need. It satisfies external needs, internal needs, and most importantly, eternal needs. In 2 Corinthians 12:9, Jesus says, "My grace is sufficient for you, for my power is made perfect in weakness."

When I don't get the promotion at work, *only grace can satisfy.*
When I do get the promotion at work, *only grace can satisfy.*
When my daughter is born, *only grace can satisfy.*
When I lose my mother to cancer, *only grace can satisfy.*
When the Yankees beat the Sox in game 7, *only grace can satisfy.*
When my son scores a goal in Little League, *only grace can satisfy.*
When, as a missionary, I've seen no converts, *only grace can satisfy.*
When my church is growing faster than ever, *only grace can satisfy.*
When condemned to hell for my sinful nature, *only grace can satisfy.*
When finally at the gates of heaven, *only grace can satisfy.*

As a side note, if you look back at this list, every time you see the word *grace* you can replace it with the words *Jesus Christ*, and it will continue to be completely true. This is true in all of scripture. Sufficiency of grace and sufficiency of Christ is proclaimed throughout the Bible. The reason being Christ and grace are one in the same. Grace cannot exist without Christ; Christ cannot exist without grace. In fact, Jesus never even used the word *grace*. He didn't have to. He personified it. Jesus, you're more than enough, yet I can't get enough.

Your Grace Is Sufficient

Your grace is sufficient for me,
Your strength is made perfect when I am weak.
And all that I cling to
I lay at your feet
Your grace is sufficient for me.[1]

Be still. Listen to what God is saying to you.

1. The word *addict* usually suggests something negative, but obviously in this chapter we are talking about a good thing called a *grace addict*. In what ways is this good?

2. Write a sentence about yourself explaining how you can't get enough of God's grace (our addiction to grace).

3. Write a sentence about yourself explaining how God's grace is more than enough for you (the sufficiency of grace).

4. Complete these thoughts:
   When I am victorious in ________________ only his grace satisfies.
   When I am disappointed in ________________ only his grace satisfies.
   When ________________ completely fails me, only his grace satisfies.

Lord, I thank you that today your grace is *comforting* me in these areas:

Lord, I thank you that today your grace is *convicting* me in these areas:

Lord, I thank you that today your grace is *calling* me to:

Today's Memory Verses: Ephesians 2:1-6

Dangers, toils, & snares

"And you were dead in the trespasses and sins in which you once walked, following the course of this world, following the prince of the power of the air, the spirit that is now at work in the sons of disobedience—among whom we all once lived in the passions of our flesh, carrying out the desires of the body and the mind, and were by nature children of wrath, like the rest of mankind. But God, being rich in mercy, because of the great love with which he loved us, even when we were dead in our trespasses, made us alive together with Christ—by grace you have been saved—and raised us up with him and seated us with him in the heavenly places in Christ Jesus, so that in the coming ages he might show the immeasurable riches of his grace in kindness toward us in Christ Jesus. For by grace you have been saved through faith. And this is not your own doing; it is the gift of God, not a result of works, so that no one may boast. For we are his workmanship, created in Christ Jesus for good works, which God prepared beforehand, that we should walk in them."

(Ephesians 2:1-10)

They say mood swings, early morning cravings, and water retention are all part of pregnancy. That couldn't have been truer than while being pregnant with our daughter, Rebecca Grace. Not for Jennifer as much as for me. Boy, did I stay bloated those days!

During the fifth month of our pregnancy (and I use the word "our" loosely), we knew that if we were going to go out of the country on vacation, this was going to be our last chance for a very long time. So, we used free air miles and headed to London to see Wimbledon. After a few days in London, Delta let us know that our return flight had been changed due to scheduling problems. This provided us the opportunity to stay a few extra days and to return home from Paris instead of London. The plan was simple: take the Chunnel to Paris for a couple of days and then fly home. As soon as plans were finalized, the first words out of Jennifer's mouth were, "Mmmmm, Paris—croissants! I think the baby is craving some!"

Needless to say, once we arrived in Paris, every outing revolved around the search for the perfect croissant. On our last morning, I woke up ridiculously early and quietly slipped out in an attempt to surprise my wife with a hot fresh croissant when she woke up. Leaving the hotel around four in the morning, with the sun yet up, I figured, *I'm in Paris, how far away from a bakery can I possibly be?*

Three lefts, two rights, another left, another right,

and thirty minutes later, I was as lost as Charleton Heston at a gun-control rally. As lost as Michael Moore at a G. W. Bush fund-raiser, as lost as Kobe Br—well, you know what I'm saying!! Somehow, I had wandered so far off the beaten path that I was on the edge of the red light district. The street I accidentally ended up on was lined with prostitutes and topless bars. The women were yelling out to me in French, and although I did not understand what they were saying, I'm sure it had nothing to do with a croissant. I quickly decided to get away, so I tried to backtrack the way I thought I had come. Somehow, however, I ended up on a street filled with even more pornography. (Have you noticed the reoccurring theme of my horrible sense of direction popping up all over this book?) What was I going to do? I didn't even have my WWJD bracelet on!

In moments like this, I would love to say that preachers are exempt from temptation, but the reality is that's not true. Maybe that's way too honest. Maybe you want to think ministers live lives of perfection, where every day is spent memorizing Leviticus and singing "Kum Ba Yah." But in real life, there is real temptation. *Temptation* is a craving or desire for something that is wrong. Temptation itself is not the sin. Giving in to the temptation is the sin. That morning, I confess, I found myself in a place of temptation. The safeguards of human accountability were nowhere to be found. I knew no one would recognize me there and my wife was in the hotel asleep. However, even though there was no physical accountability, there was an even-greater truth that sustained me—Jesus. It is the sufficiency of God's grace that allows us to walk away from temptation. When I live in the reality of what Christ did on the cross to defeat sin in my life (grace), it enables me to see sin for what it really is: a momentary pleasure with destructive intentions.

When we give in to temptation, we are saying to ourselves, *I do not believe in the promises of God. Sure, God promises me that through his grace, he can satisfy my every need, but I don't believe it. I need to commit this momentary sin to make me happy.*

What keeps me faithful in moments like this is not my marriage or even my call to ministry, but the reality that my sufficiency is found in Christ. His grace is sufficient to sustain me. Much bigger than my call to be faithful to my wife, or my call to ministry, is my call to be faithful to my God.

What if my wife had been really mean to me that morning? Then could I have condoned sinning? What if I knew 100 percent that no one would find out and my ministerial reputation would not be affected? Then could I have condoned it? After all, I didn't go looking for it; it came looking for me. I'm just a victim, right? NO! All of these excuses are null and void if my satisfaction is fully found in Jesus.

Show me a sex addict, and I'll show you someone who has not found his complete satisfaction in the grace of God. Show me someone addicted to money, and I'll show you someone who is trying to feel satisfied with material things. Show me a church addict, someone who fills her life with Christian activity instead of with Christ, and I'll show you someone who has succumbed to temptation as well. When Jesus Christ was in the desert (Matthew 4), he was tempted by Satan, yet did not sin.

Jesus used scripture to rebuke Satan, teaching us one practical way to fight the enemy. James 4:7 says, "Submit yourselves therefore to God. Resist the devil, and he will flee from you." Another practical way to prepare for the "dark alleys" of the world is to establish a well-beaten path in our lives through spiritual disciplines like Bible study and prayer. Let me illustrate. A few years ago, we lived in a house that backed up to a tennis club. I would daily climb the little hill in our backyard and hop on over to the courts to play. I did this so much that eventually my footsteps had created a well-beaten path. This turned out to be useful on the evenings that I would finish a long match and need the path to guide me home in the dark. As a matter of fact, I had so memorized the way that I could do it with my eyes closed. This illustrates why spiritual disciplines like scripture memorization are such a vital part of growing in grace. They will lead you home, even in the dark!

In case you were wondering, that's just what happened to me that morning in Paris. Because I had previously created a well-worn path in my life by daily spending time in God's Word, I was spiritually prepared for the temptation that awaited me in that dark moment. There in the red light district at 4:30 in the morning, the Word of God became living and active in me. I began to recite the passage in Hebrews 12:14 that says, "Without holiness no one will see the Lord" (NIV). As I repeated that passage over and over again, I finally found my way out of that neighborhood and eventually made my way back to our hotel. I had failed in providing Jennifer a croissant, but I had succeeded in winning a much bigger battle. With Jennifer still sleeping, I slipped quietly into the room and thanked God that his grace was sufficient for me.

Amazing Grace
Through many dangers, toils, and snares
I have already come.
'Tis grace has brought me safe thus far,
And grace will lead me home.[1]

Be Still. Listen to what God is saying to you.

1. What is temptation?

2. How do we know that it is not a sin to be tempted?

3. What are some weapons used to fight temptation (prayer, etc.)? List three or four. Which ones are defensive and which are offensive? How are you using these weapons to effectively fight off temptation?

4. Journal about a recent scenario when you were able to walk in the sufficiency of God's grace in the midst of temptation.

Lord, I thank you that today your grace is *comforting* me in these areas:

Lord, I thank you that today your grace is *convicting* me in these areas:

Lord, I thank you that today your grace is *calling* me to:

Today's Memory Verses: Ephesians 2:1-6

A Click of the Chin

One of my greatest regrets is that I did not get to know Jeff Bannon better. The first time I met Jeff, he was already paralyzed and unable to speak. A ventilator filled his lungs with air, while a feeding tube pumped nourishment into his stomach. When I walked into his house, my eyes met Jeff's eyes and I instantly saw a joy that overcame his circumstances. Jeff was in the latter stages of ALS, amyotrophic lateral sclerosis, commonly known as Lou Gehrig's disease, a disease that over time will paralyze every muscle in the human body. A former athlete who had biked through Europe and was on his college wrestling team, Jeff was now only able to communicate through a computer operated by the slight movement of his chin. When God gifted Jeff by enrolling him in the school of suffering, he enrolled his family as well. Having a handicapped person in your family can affect every avenue of your life. Relentless time demands and never-ending medical costs create a lot of stress. Thankfully, Jeff and his family had a support system—their friends and their church. The afternoon I met Jeff, his sweet wife, Jodie, and their son, Jeffery, I saw a beautiful family portrait of the power of God's sufficient grace. Jeff communicated more grace with just a few clicks of his chin on his computer than most people do in a lifetime.

A couple years later I received a call from my brother-in-law Cary. Weeping, he told me Jeff would be taken off the ventilator the next morning. After ten years of physical decline resulting in excruciating pain and total paralysis, Jeff's body had worn out. The joy over Jeff's final release from Lou Gehrig's disease, yet the painful loss of such a great man, was a bittersweet reality. As we talked on the phone, Cary mentioned that over the past few months Jeff had repeatedly requested to hear the modern anthem about heaven, "I Can Only Imagine." Jeff loved the song because, although he would miss his family and friends on earth, it reminded him of the hope of heaven. As soon as Cary and I got off the phone, I put in a call to Bart Millard, the lead singer of MercyMe and writer of "I Can Only Imagine."

When told about Jeff's situation and his love for the song, Bart graciously called Jeff to sing the song over him by speakerphone. Later, Bart told me that even though he called to minister to Jeff and his family, he himself had ended up being the one ministered to the most. Jeff always exhibited grace under tremendous circumstances and affected everyone he met.

On June 2, 2004, Jeff entered the gates of heaven. Ironically, the day of his death fell on the same day as the death of Lou Gehrig. There was no funeral. Instead, there was a service of celebration. The church was packed as family and friends gathered to honor a man who had not let his physical handicap dampen his soaring spirit.

"My flesh and my heart may fail, but God is the strength of my heart and my portion forever" (Psalm 73:26).

Wild at Heart author John Eldredge never met Jeff, but after hearing his story had this to say in an e-mail: "Hearing Jeff's story, I was speechless. Here was a man of courage, strength, and a brave, brave heart. I wish I could be like him. Jeff proved that the heart is boundless and free."

Grace Extension

In many ways, Jeff Bannon was the exception to the rule. Jeff was blessed with a strong network of friends and family who were always willing to come and lend a hand. Sadly, this is not the case for many of the physically or mentally challenged. I know of very few churches that have taken strategic steps to minister to the mentally and physically handicapped. We, as the church, need to stop being afraid to serve those who have disabilities. Last year my family's home church allowed my brother Benjamin to be a part of their softball league. For many players on the team, this was inconvenient to say the least. Every time Benjamin stepped up to the plate, he mysteriously hit a home run. Have you ever seen anyone bat a thousand? Well, I sure did! To me, Benjamin wasn't the only one who batted one thousand that season. These Christian athletes (on both sides of the field) befriended my brother and allowed him to be a part of the game. Every single time Benjamin went up to bat, both teams would begin to cheer. This happened every game, every single time he batted. Benjamin would proceed to bunt the ball, then run and slide into first base. Without fail, the ball would be overthrown to the first baseman, and Benjamin would start his run and slide routine around the diamond. Mark McGwire might have had Creatine, but Benjamin had something far greater. He belonged to a church softball league that was all about extending the grace of God. Here are some other ideas on how to be an extender of that kind of grace:

1. Get a book transcribed into Braille for someone who is blind.

2. Volunteer with the Special Olympics.

3. If you are handy with tools, get together some friends and make a physically handicapped person's house more accessible (i.e., build a ramp, widen a doorway, lower a sink, etc.).

4. Plan a girl's night out with some young girls who are physically or mentally handicapped. Let their family drop them off, allowing the parents a night off. Maybe use the fellowship hall of the church. Give manicures, style hair, or even paint toenails. Create a fun night for some special girls while their parents and siblings get a night away.

5. Under the accountability of your church, raise funds for the handicapped in your area or financially support great organizations such as www.alsironhorse.org. Jeff Bannon and his family founded the Ironhorse Foundation and extend grace to those in need.

Be Involved!

Today's Memory Verses: Ephesians 2:1-7

Lord, I thank you that today your grace is *comforting* me in these areas:

Lord, I thank you that today your grace is *convicting* me in these areas:

Lord, I thank you that today your grace is *calling* me to:

Today's Memory Verses: Ephesians 2:1-7

Whatever my lot

*"And you were dead in the trespasses and sins in which you once walked, following the prince of the power of the air, the spirit that is now at work in the sons of disobedience—among whom we all once lived in the passions of our flesh, carrying out the desires of the body and the mind, and were by nature children of wrath, like the rest of mankind. But God, being rich in mercy, because of the great love with which he loved us, even when we were dead in our trespasses, made us alive together with Christ—**by grace** you have been saved—and raised us up with him and seated us with him in the heavenly places in Christ Jesus, so that in the coming ages he might show the immeasurable riches of his grace in kindness toward us in Christ Jesus. For by grace you have been saved through faith. And this is not your own doing; it is the gift of God, not a result of works, so that no one may boast. For we are his workmanship, created in Christ Jesus for good works, which God prepared beforehand, that we should walk in them." (Ephesians 2:1-10)*

Horatio Spafford stood on the deck of the ship and stared down into the cold, dark sea. Just a few days before, his four daughters had drowned as their ship sank in these same freezing waters. He had sent his wife and daughters ahead of him on a ship bound for the United Kingdom, and had planned to join them in England a few days after they landed. He sensed his family needed a vacation after enduring the hardest few years of their lives. They had lost their fortune due to the Great Chicago Fire of 1871, and as a family they had mourned the loss of their four-year-old boy due to scarlet fever. As a father, I cannot imagine what was going through his mind.

Horatio was a man of faith who grasped the sufficiency of grace even in the midst of suffering. That cold December night, the captain told Horatio they were passing over the spot he believed to be the place where the 226 people had drowned, including Horatio's daughters. It was that very night Horatio began to pen one of the greatest hymns of all time, "It Is Well with My Soul." In Psalm 34:18-19, the psalmist proclaims, "The Lord is near to the brokenhearted and saves the crushed in spirit. Many are the afflictions of the righteous, but the Lord delivers him out of them all."

It is one thing to profess the wellness of your soul when all the circumstances of your life are on an upswing. However, for Horatio Spafford, that song was birthed out of tremendous tragedy. Horatio understood that hardship and trials are a part of life. There is no escaping them. In life, the question is not *if* I ever go through suffering, but *when*. Jesus tells us in John 16:33 that "in this world you will have trouble" (NIV). Great theologian Charles Spurgeon once said, "The path of sorrow has been trodden by thousands of holy feet; you are not the only one, and you will not be the last one."[1] Think about it. You will probably mourn the loss of your parents one day, if you have not already. If you do not mourn theirs, then they will likely mourn yours. Sorrow is inevitable. When the days of suffering come, it is the sufficiency of grace that will carry us through.

No one likes to suffer. From the day we are born, we try to run from hardship and pain. So much effort is put into insulating our lives from any discomfort, whether physical or emotional. When suffering does come, however, we can easily fall into the trap of thinking that God is punishing us by allowing this to happen, and that he has removed his hand of blessing. *God, what did I do wrong to deserve this?* is a question frequently asked in the midst of hardship. We may think to ourselves, *If God loves me, then why would he want me to suffer? If he allows me to suffer, he's taken away his hand of blessing and is probably upset with me.* These mistaken thoughts are birthed out of the idea that grace and suffering cannot go hand-in-hand. We think hardship equals wrath, and ease equals grace.

Biblically, however, this is far from the truth. In fact, it is very evident throughout all of scripture that the grace of God is poured out through suffering. Suffering creates character (James 1). When the circumstances of our lives are bigger than us, we can learn many lessons about relying on Christ alone to meet our every need. No one can read the Bible and deny that God ordains suffering for those he loves as a means of extending grace to and through those circumstances. Whether it is Moses in the desert, Daniel in the lions' den, David in the cave, or Mary in the barn, it is the sufficiency of God's grace that is woven throughout their stories. We see their suffering produce endurance, their endurance produce character, and their character produce hope. As illustrated in Romans 5:3-5, the lives of these saints have become a testimony that the grace of God is more than enough, no matter what.

Maybe you're wondering why God allows suffering in the lives of Christians. The Bible offers many reasons for this. One is to remind us that if we put our trust and happiness in anything the world has to offer, we will fail. Paul explains in 2 Corinthians 1:8, "For we were so utterly burdened beyond our strength that we despaired of life itself. Indeed, we felt that we had received the sentence of death. But that was to make us rely not on ourselves but on God who raises the dead." Nothing in this fallen world can satisfy. Obtain all the money and friends in the world, but if your best friend tragically drowns, praying to a bank account will not provide peace and assurance. In that moment of suffering, only Christ can meet your deepest need.

Another reason God allows Christians to suffer is to display Christ's peace in the midst of storms. "But even if you should suffer for righteousness' sake, you will be blessed...always being prepared to make a defense to anyone who asks you for a reason for the hope that is in you" (1 Peter 3:14-15). There is no greater testimony of the sufficiency of his grace than to see it lived out moment by moment, in the life of a believer who is going through tough times.

God also allows suffering to come in order to help us identify more with Christ. To share in his sufferings is to be in union with Christ. Paul shares this idea in Philippians 3:10: "That I may know him and the power of his resurrection, and may share his sufferings, becoming like him in his death." As we join together with Christ in suffering, we can fully appreciate the suffering he endured on our behalf.

One final reason God allows difficult times in a believer's life is so the circumstance can become used as a tool to deepen and refine our faith. This is part of the process of growing in grace. "And after you have suffered a little while, the God of all grace, who has called you to his eternal glory in Christ, will himself restore, confirm, strengthen, and establish you" (1 Peter 5:10).

Job was a godly man who went through terrible hardship and pain. Much like Horatio Spafford, he lost his fortune and his family. On top of this, he even contracted a very painful skin disease. Job's wife and friends misunderstood why God was allowing such suffering to come his way. Even so, Job became a testimony to them that God's grace was enough to carry him, even in the midst of hell on earth. What I love about the book of Job is the honesty of his struggle. We don't see a man who has it all figured out. We see a man who is struggling to make sense of it all but who, nevertheless, understands that God has a bigger plan than what is in front of him. Job pronounced in chapter 23, "But he knows the way that I take; when he has tried me, I shall come out as gold." Even though Job probably never knew all the reasons behind his painful circumstances, he seemed to understand that God allows grief to highlight the sufficiency of his grace. James even reflects on Job's faithfulness in suffering: "Behold, we consider those blessed who remained steadfast. You have heard of the steadfastness of Job, and you have seen the purpose of the Lord, how the Lord is compassionate and merciful" (James 5:11).

If you are reading this today and you're going through serious hard times, know that God is always good and his grace is always sufficient. If you're not experiencing any trials, bookmark this chapter and more importantly, saturate yourself with God's Word because one day "sea billows will roll."

It Is Well with My Soul
When peace, like a river, attendeth my way,
When sorrows like sea billows roll;
Whatever my lot, Thou has taught me to say,
It is well, it is well with my soul.[2]

Be Still. Listen to what God is saying to you.

1. Finish this sentence: It is well with my soul even though...

2. What are some reasons that God allows suffering in your life? How can suffering be a blessing and not a curse?

3. What can be learned and what growth can develop from suffering?

4. Do you know anyone who is going through a really hard time? Write a prayer specifically for that person. Consider what God would have you do to encourage that person.

5. Why is it important to establish good theology about suffering, even during the mountaintop moments of life?

Lord, I thank you that today your grace is *comforting* me in these areas:

Lord, I thank you that today your grace is *convicting* me in these areas:

Lord, I thank you that today your grace is *calling* me to:

Today's Memory Verses: Ephesians 2:1-7

Sonny & share

*"And you were dead in the trespasses and sins in which you once walked, following the prince of the power of the air, the spirit that is now at work in the sons of disobedience—among whom we all once lived in the passions of our flesh, carrying out the desires of the body and the mind, and were by nature children of wrath, like the rest of mankind. But God, being rich in mercy, because of the great love with which he loved us, even when we were dead in our trespasses, made us alive together with Christ—**by grace** you have been saved—and raised us up with him and seated us with him in the heavenly places in Christ Jesus, so that in the coming ages he might show the immeasurable riches of his grace in kindness toward us in Christ Jesus. For by grace you have been saved through faith. And this is not your own doing; it is the gift of God, not a result of works, so that no one may boast. For we are his workmanship, created in Christ Jesus for good works, which God prepared beforehand, that we should walk in them."*

(Ephesians 2:1-10)

And the award for the cheesiest chapter title in the history of books goes to...(drum roll, please)... David Nasser for calling his chapter on the sufficiency of grace in evangelism "Sonny & Share." I know, I know, but I just couldn't help it! While I'm being extremely cheesy, allow me to make my point. If our lives are lived in the "Son," then we are compelled to "share" the good news of his grace. In other words, if we are "Sonny," then we will "share"—OK, OK, I'll stop.

Notice that I did not say in order to be "Sonny," we must "share." I said *if* we are "Sonny," *then* we will "share." To be "Sonny" is to be full of the Son of God; not just full to the top, but full to the point of overflowing. Evangelism is not something we do to receive God's grace but rather something we do because of God's amazing grace overflowsing in our lives. If we have received the saving grace of God, we can't help but share it with others. The news is too good to keep just for us. As believers, we are commanded in the Great Commission to go into the entire world and proclaim the gospel. In fact, the definition of the word *evangelism*, taken from the Greek, means, "to announce good news." Today, we are going to look at three "if we believe" statements that should encourage those of us who are "Sonny" to "share." (This is the last time I bring up the "Sonny & Share" thing...hopefully!)

If we believe that God's grace is sufficient to save us, then we must also believe it is enough to save others. In true evangelism, the message is centered on God's unmerited favor. Period. To preach that changed behavior earns (merits) God's favor is to say that God's grace is not sufficient. Works-based evangelism discounts what Christ did on the cross. We are not called to be the behavior police of the world; we are called to be proclaimers of the truth. And the truth of the gospel is that salvation is only found through the completed work of Jesus Christ. Romans 11:6 says, "But if it is by grace, it is no longer on the basis of works; otherwise grace would no longer be grace." In other words, we cannot ask a lost world to change their behavior so that God will accept them.

Paul also states in Titus 2:11-12, "For the grace of God has appeared, bringing salvation for all people, training us to renounce ungodliness and worldly passions, and to live self-controlled, upright, and godly lives in the present age." This means it is the work of God's grace *in* us that causes us to change our behavior once we have received Christ. It is acceptable to use works to point out the symptoms that signify an eternal disease, as long as we don't get caught up in only treating the symptoms. In presenting the kindness and severity of God (Romans 11) to a lost world, we must not get bogged down with behavior modification. To major on the major is to major on grace.

If we believe God's grace is sufficient, then we are victorious when we share the gospel, no matter the outcome. We are victorious simply because we obey. Paul encourages us in 2 Timothy chapter four to "preach the Word; be ready in season and out of season...do the work of an evangelist." If the person I'm witnessing to receives Christ, then God's grace is sufficient through me. But if the person walks away, then his grace is still sufficient for me. I am simply called to be obedient and let God take care of the outcome.

I remember going to bed many nights praying for my father's salvation. Time after time, I had seen him reject the gospel. Many times I messed up in my delivery of God's salvation plan. Other times my dad had seen major failure in my own Christian walk, and he often used this as an excuse not to accept Christ. Romans 9:16 says, "So then it depends not on human will or exertion, but on God, who has mercy." Eventually, my father did become a Christian. The victory was twofold. My father came to a saving knowledge of Christ, and my personal walk with the Lord was enriched as I walked in obedience to Jesus' command to share the gospel. Theologian Wayne Grudem says, "Evangelism is a means of grace, then, not only in the sense that it administers grace to the unsaved, but also because those who evangelize experience more of the Holy Spirit's presence and blessing in their own lives."[1] David Nasser was insufficient, but God's grace was more than enough.

If we believe that God's grace is sufficient, then we can share the gospel with those who are not gracious to us. We do not have to like certain people, but in God's grace and strength we are commanded to love them. A few neighborhoods ago, Jennifer and I had a neighbor who obviously did not like me. In all honesty, the feeling was mutual. The main problem was his dog. On Tuesday mornings we usually woke up to the beeping sound of the garbage truck backing up in front of our house. On more than one occasion, I would run out with a garbage bag, only to find trash covering our front lawn. The neighbor's dog loved digging in the trash bags of everyone in the cul-de-sac, and he would bring the trash, piece by piece, into my yard. This happened all the time and created some serious issues.

Issue number one: There is a leash law, and this neighbor chose to ignore it.

Issue number two: It is embarrassing for a preacher to be picking up his neighbor's beer cans off his lawn at seven in the morning, while waving to teenagers as they are driving to school.

Issue number three: Although I appreciated the free fertilizer left behind by his dog, when told, my neighbor couldn't have cared less.

One Tuesday morning, the yard was completely trashed. After cleaning up the mess, I came back into the house and lay down fuming. Thoughts of hot dogs and antifreeze were rolling around in my head. Jennifer must have read my mind, because she immediately turned over and said, "What's the matter?"

I replied, "Well, sweetie, other than your morning breath, the dog trashed our yard again."

Then I lost it. I went off into a rant about my neighbor and all the problems I had with him. When I wound down, Jennifer sat up in bed and said the last thing I wanted to hear. "Why don't we pray for him? You start, David."

What? She wanted me to pray for him?! That was the last thing I wanted to do. But Jennifer wouldn't give up. She reminded me he was not a Christian and how, instead of being angry, we should pray for God to change our hearts. As we prayed, the insufficiency of my neighbor and the insufficiency of my love for him were overshadowed by the sufficiency of God's grace. My heart went from anger to brokenness. Jesus commands us in Luke 6:27-28, "Love your enemies, do good to those who hate you, bless those who curse you, pray for those who abuse you." How could anyone even attempt to do this apart from the miracle-working grace of God?

Think about it. Did God love us because we were so lovable? No. Jesus does not ask us to love the unlovable without first setting that example for us. In Jesus' life, we see him loving not only the disciples but also the Roman soldiers who nailed him to the cross. His words were brokenhearted and not angry when he said, "Father, forgive them, for they know not what they do" (Luke 23:34). I am in no way saying that what I went through with my neighbor or what you may be going through today compares to what Christ went through on the cross. However, no matter how large or small the evangelistic challenge we face, God's grace is more than enough.

Be Still. Listen to what God is saying to you.

1. What is evangelism and why should it be not a chore, but a gift?

2. Why is it so difficult to share our faith with the lost? Be specific. List the fears and emotions experienced in witnessing.

3. If the grace message is enough in evangelism, why do we focus more on behavior change than the reality of God's grace?

4. Why is it that we are still victorious whenever we share the gospel even if the person rejects the truth?

5. Write down the initials of four people you do not like. (Before you throw my name in the pot, remember that I have already apologized for the cheesy titles within this book!)

6. Write a prayer asking God to soften your heart toward those you listed. Choose one and demonstrate grace to them.

Lord, I thank you that today your grace is *comforting* me in these areas:

Lord, I thank you that today your grace is *convicting* me in these areas:

Lord, I thank you that today your grace is *calling* me to:

Today's Memory Verses: Ephesians 2:1-7

Orphans to heirs

*"And you were dead in the trespasses and sins in which you once walked, following the prince of the power of the air, the spirit that is now at work in the sons of disobedience—among whom we all once lived in the passions of our flesh, carrying out the desires of the body and the mind, and were by nature children of wrath, like the rest of mankind. But God, being rich in mercy, because of the great love with which he loved us, even when we were dead in our trespasses, made us alive together with Christ—by grace you have been saved—**and raised us up with him and seated us with him in the heavenly places in Christ Jesus,** so that in the coming ages he might show the immeasurable riches of his grace in kindness toward us in Christ Jesus. For by grace you have been saved through faith. And this is not your own doing; it is the gift of God, not a result of works, so that no one may boast. For we are his workmanship, created in Christ Jesus for good works, which God prepared beforehand, that we should walk in them."*
(Ephesians 2:1-10)

"If this thing ever really gets serious, I need you to know that I can only marry a man who is excited about adopting children one day." When Jennifer made this statement early in our relationship, I wanted so badly to keep dating her I responded with something like, "Oh, yeah, sure, that sounds great." What I didn't realize at the time was she was completely serious.

As a seven-year-old, on a first-grade fieldtrip, Jennifer was profoundly impacted by the Charles Dickens movie *Oliver Twist.* God used it to tenderize her heart toward orphans all over the world. Jennifer's passion for these children didn't stop when we were dating, or when we married, or even when we had our daughter, Grace. It only increased.

Then after eight years of marriage, God prepared my heart for the same. Two years later, Rudy Nasser joined our family. This amazing seven-year-old boy from Guatemala is a daily affirmation, of not only the beauty of physical adoption but the life-changing work of spiritual adoption.

Spiritual adoption is the act by which God allows us to become members of his family. Through spiritual adoption, God makes us his children. Through Christ's completed work on the cross, we receive right standing with God through justification. *Justification* is a legal term. It implies that justice has been served, and that we are in right legal standing before God.

Our sin and guilt are forgiven. *Adoption*, however, is much more personal than justification. *Adoption* is a family term. Although through justification we are forgiven, through adoption we are embraced by God and become his heirs. It implies love and acceptance.

Author J. I. Packer observes, "To be right with God the judge is a great thing, but to be loved and cared for by God is greater."[1] If God wanted to simply save us through justification by faith, then he could have stopped there. But he didn't. God has not only saved us, but he has also taken us in and made us a part of his family. Think about it. Jennifer and I could have saved Rudy from a life of poverty and hardship in Guatemala by paying for a good home, an education, food, and all his debts, all without giving him the benefit of our last name. That is called *sponsorship* and it's a good thing. It is something entirely different to bring him to our home, hand him the keys, give him our name, and say, "It's all yours. You are now one of us." That is essentially what spiritual adoption does.

If justification makes Jesus Christ our Savior, then adoption makes us joint heirs with him. In Ephesians 2:6, Paul refers to this truth when he says that God "raised us up with him and seated us with him in the heavenly places in Christ Jesus." Again in Romans 8:16-17, Paul writes, "The Spirit himself bears witness with our spirit that we are children of God, and if children, then heirs—heirs of God and fellow heirs with Christ." We go from the orphanage to the mansion.

I remember the day we told Rudy he was our son. It was 9:00 a.m. in Guatemala and the adoption attorney brought him to our hotel so we could spend the day together. We had never met him, and we were scared to death. Before Jennifer and I left our room, we looked over our balcony into the indoor atrium. There sat Rudy on a couch looking very tiny and waiting for us. I could only see the top of his head, Jennifer saw even more: with hair parted on one side and slicked down as if trying to put his best foot forward, Jennifer knew immediately that this was her son. We prayed all the way down in the elevator. With one look at him, we both had an overwhelming confirmation in our spirits. After spending the day together, we were all weeping when it was time to part. Jennifer and I were crying because we felt as if we were leaving our son behind in Guatemala; Rudy was crying because he thought we did not want him. The second we realized he was so sad, we quickly assured him that, although we had to go back to America, we would not rest until the day he could make the journey with us. As I hugged Rudy good-bye, I told him, "You are now part of our family. You are my son." At that moment for Jennifer and me, it was more binding than any adoption certificate. Although in our hearts Rudy was our son and we were his parents, it was twenty-one more months before we were actually able to bring him home. Although Rudy wasn't physically with us during those long twenty-one months, he was still our son. We prepared his room, bought him clothes, wrote him letters, and signed him up for an Upward Soccer team. He was just as much our son then as he is now that he is here with us.

Paul gives us that exact same hope here in Ephesians two. He is reminding us that although we are not, at this moment, physically seated in the heavenly places with Christ, we can hold fast to the hope that one day we will be eternally there. We become heirs of the promise. Charles Spurgeon claims, "The first born alone was enough to fill the father's heart throughout eternity. And yet the Lord puts us among the children. Blessed be his name forever and ever!"[2] "Behold what manner of love the father has bestowed on us, that we should be called children of God" (1 John 3:1 NKJV).

Getting back to Upward Soccer, as I am writing this chapter Rudy just finished his last game of the season. I saw my son score a goal and immediately turn his eyes to the sidelines as if to say, "Did you see that, Daddy?" To Rudy, I am Daddy. I am not guardian, sponsor, or even adopted father. I am Daddy. He has the confidence that I will love him, and he will always be able to call me Daddy, no matter what happens in his life. He feels free to bring me his victories, defeats, needs, and wants. He is confident that I will listen and will always do what is best for him. He did not feel this way about me when I was a stranger, only after I became Daddy. No other children but my own call me Daddy. This is what Christ called God in the Garden of Gethsemane, and it is what we can call God today. Abba, Father...Daddy.

Adoption is the personalization of our faith. Through God's grace, demonstrated through adoption, we are able to approach God freely and with confidence. Hebrews 4:16 makes known, "Let us then with confidence draw near to the throne of grace, that we may receive mercy, and find grace to help in time of need." Paul reinforces this in Romans 8:15-16: "For you did not receive the spirit of slavery to fall back into fear, but you have received the Spirit of adoption as sons, by whom we cry, 'Abba! Father!' The Spirit himself bears witness with our spirit that we are children of God."

In Mark Stibbe's book *Orphans to Heirs*, he encourages us to pray this prayer daily. I think it is a beautiful conclusion:

God's Word tells me that I'm an adopted child of God and that I'm infinitely loved. Holy Spirit, I welcome you into my life afresh today. Please bring a new revelation to my spirit that Abba, Father loves me for who I am and not for what I do. Please place me once again under the affirming radiance of the Father's smile. Amen.[3]

Be still. Listen to what God is saying to you.

1. Define spiritual orphan and spiritual heir.

2. What would our relationship to God be like if we were justified but not his children?

3. How does the reality of our adoption through grace affect the way we act toward each other as a family of God?

4. Are there any instances where you have been territorial or selfish and not family-oriented?

Lord, I thank you that today your grace is *comforting* me in these areas:

Lord, I thank you that today your grace is *convicting* me in these areas:

Lord, I thank you that today your grace is *calling* me to:

Today's Memory Verse: Ephesians 2:1-7

Grace & Chicken Pox

People who have gone through deep valleys of hurt often become people who draw from a deeper well of insight. This couldn't be truer than in the life of one of my best friends.

Joel and I met in a trailer. We were both at a youth camp and Joel was staying in the camp trailer during the week. He had on a bright yellow shirt and a hat that had the word *Frap* on it. At first glance, it didn't seem as if we would be two guys who would hit it off. But by the end of the week, I knew that there was something exceptional about this worship leader, and that we would become lifelong friends.

Joel Craddick was raised in San Francisco by a single mom. Joel and his mom were close, even though she had a lot of personal problems that affected him emotionally. He never knew his dad. When Joel was just a young kid, his mom suffered a stroke, and four days later passed away. He was sent to live with his elderly grandparents in a tiny town in Oklahoma. Talk about culture shock! Joel's grandparents took him in, but life for Joel seemed to get even harder. On several occasions I have heard Joel speak of his struggles during those days in Oklahoma. He had come from San Francisco, California, to Enid, Oklahoma. On top of that, he was living with two senior citizens who were having a hard time taking care of themselves, much less a rambunctious young boy. Joel was fourteen when his grandfather died. His grandmother had to go to a retirement home, so Joel packed his bags and took himself to the local Baptist Children's Home. "Life was basically miserable for me. I was constantly afraid of what was going to happen to me. I felt so alone, unloved, and unhappy. However, God was moving in my life, and most of the time I was unaware of it. That's often how he works," says Joel looking back.

One day, when chicken pox broke out at the Children's Home, the director contacted Dale and Nadine Engle to see if Joel could come stay with them temporarily. They had helped out with kids in the past, and agreed that Joel could come until the chicken pox went away. I want to stop at this point, lift my hands, and say a big "Hallelujah!" for chicken pox. "And we know that for those who love God all things work together for good, for those who are called according to his purpose" (Romans 8:28).

The Engles fell in love with Joel, and Joel fell in love with the Engles. So, at the age of sixteen, Joel became a social-work miracle and was adopted by the Engle family. Joel recalls one afternoon in which he was sent home from school after getting into a big fight. Joel feared the Engles would return him to the Children's Home. However, when Mrs. Engle came in the room and sat by Joel, she told him that there was nothing he could ever do that would stop him from being their son. "If God had not placed my mom and dad in my life, I would probably not be alive today. Through their Christlike attitude, I finally felt loved and secure. I knew I needed to solidify my relationship with Jesus Christ, so when I was sixteen I received Christ and I have never been the same," says Joel. It was through his adoption that God changed not only Joel's last name but also his heart.

One night at camp I asked Joel when it was he began to sing and play the piano. He told me he was at a church just wasting time one afternoon when he sat down at the piano bench in the sanctuary. Looking at the piano, Joel said, "God, if you give me the ability to play this piano, I will never play or sing for anyone but you." The rest is history. Today, Joel is one of God's anointed voices for this generation. I have seen him lead worship with crowds of fifteen and fifteen thousand. One of our camp experiences together at Falls Creek was unforgettable. Since the camp was in Oklahoma, Joel's parents drove up to see their son sing and lead. I sat in the second row, right behind Dale and Nadine Engle. I saw Nadine weep as Joel sang about the power of God's amazing grace. I wept, too, as I thought about how God took a little boy through so much grit and grace so he could bring him to this beautiful place. What a portrait of grace. Praise God for chicken pox!!!

Grace Extension

Our world is a world full of hurting children. An average of 35,000 people lose their lives to starvation every day around the world. In third-world countries like Botswana, Africa, nearly four in ten adults are infected with the AIDS virus. Children wake up every morning with absolutely no one to take care of him or her. To date, almost 15 million children have lost their parents to the AIDS pandemic. In 1990 UNICEF estimatee that there are 210 million orphans currently in the world. By the year 2010, it is projected that the number will rise to 240 million. Stats like this can boggle the mind. The danger in statistics is that they can become numbing and can just look like just a bunch of zeros. However, the number 210 million represents 210 million individual lives that are valuable to God. As Christians, we *must* rise up and help! It is not the job of the United Nations or the United States, but the responsibility of the United Body of Christ to be on the front lines of reacting to this unbelievable tragedy. It is a logical conclusion that we, who have received such a great grace, should be the very ones who should freely extend it. I don't believe that God is *suggesting* that we become involved in helping these children who suffer so greatly; I believe he is *requiring* it.

Today (and I don't mean next week or once you start making a big salary sometime in the future), I am pleading with you to extend the grace of God to the orphans of the world. Matthew 18:5 challenges, "Whoever receives one such child in my name receives me." In the name of Jesus, let's help these orphans who are so desperate.

You may be asking, "How do I even begin to be involved?" Well, let me suggest a few extension ideas:

One: Give your life to missions. If God is calling you to a life of mission work, surrender today. To live and minister among the poorest of the poor is to share the same address as Jesus.

Two: Take a mission trip to a developing country. If your church is not taking a trip in the near future and you desire to go and minister in these areas as an extension of grace, check out organizations such as Student Life (www.studentlife.net) and Teen Mania (www.teenmania.com). "Religion that is pure and undefiled before God, the Father, is this: to visit orphans and widows in their affliction, and to keep oneself unstained from the world" (James 1:27).

Three: If you don't sense God's call to go to another country, there are 2.6 million orphans in the United States. Many of them would love a friend who would take them to the mall, buy them a pair of shoes, and then play a game of hoops with them on a local basketball court. Maybe even contact a local children's home and offer to tutor a young child who is having trouble with math. As we saw earlier, it was the "grace extension" of the Engle family toward a teenager in the midst of a chicken pox epidemic that made all the difference. One organization that allows you to befriend and sponsor an orphan in the United States is Hope Chest (www.hopechest.org).

Four: Sponsor a child through a world-relief organization such as World Vision (www.worldvision.com) or Compassion International (www.compassioninternational.com). For around thirty dollars a month, these ministries provide you with the opportunity to feed, shelter, and clothe a child who would otherwise go without. When you feed a hungry belly, that belly is connected to a heart that wonders why you care. What a powerful "grace extension" moment. Through sponsorship ministries like World Vision, literally thousands of children come to receive Christ as Savior every year. "Open your mouth for the mute, for the rights of all who are destitute. Open your mouth, judge righteously, defend the rights of the poor and needy" (Proverbs 31:8-9).

Five: I realize this particular Grace Extension is only for a few, however by the time you get to this part of the book God may have spoken to you about adopting a child. Maybe you are young and God is affirming this as a call for your future. But maybe, just maybe, you are an adult who senses today that there is room in your family for one more. Through great ministries such as Shaohannah's Hope (www.shaohannashope.org) and Lifeline Adoption Services (www.lifelineadoption.org) you can become the turning point in a child's life.

Be Involved!

Today's Memory Verses: Ephesians 2:1-8

Lord, I thank you that today your grace is *comforting* me in these areas:

Lord, I thank you that today your grace is *convicting* me in these areas:

Lord, I thank you that today your grace is *calling* me to:

Today's Memory Verses: Ephesians 2:1-8

A war already won

*"And you were dead in the trespasses and sins in which you once walked, following the prince of the power of the air, the spirit that is now at work in the sons of disobedience—among whom we all once lived in the passions of our flesh, carrying out the desires of the body and the mind, and were by nature children of wrath, like the rest of mankind. But God, being rich in mercy, because of the great love with which he loved us, even when we were dead in our trespasses, made us alive together with Christ—by grace you have been saved—**and raised us up with him and seated us with him in the heavenly places in Christ Jesus,** so that in the coming ages he might show the immeasurable riches of his grace in kindness toward us in Christ Jesus. For by grace you have been saved through faith. And this is not your own doing; it is the gift of God, not a result of works, so that no one may boast. For we are his workmanship, created in Christ Jesus for good works, which God prepared beforehand, that we should walk in them." (Ephesians 2:1-10)*

I have never been in a green "green room." The walls are usually painted mauve or cream or some other wimpy pastel color. For those of you unfamiliar with what a "green room" is, it is the room backstage at an event where the stage personalities can relax, eat, and prepare. I remember on one occasion finding myself in a green room full of men in suits and ties. It was somewhat unusual for me because on any given night I am usually in a green room full of young guys with bleached hair, wearing tight T-shirts and overpriced jeans (a.k.a. Christian music artists). On that particular night, I had been invited to speak at a pastor's conference. Eventually, the gentleman in charge of the conference asked all the speakers to gather together in a word of prayer. It was an honor for me to join hands in prayer with some giants of the faith. I knew these men from their books, their churches, and their television and radio ministries. I have to admit, I was a little intimidated.

What happened next I will never forget. The first gentleman that began to pray cried out loud, "God, I am the biggest sinner here. I know that my brothers struggle every day, but no one fails more than I do. I'm not worthy even to be here." After he finished his prayer, the next pastor began with, "Lord, I know my brother says he is the biggest sinner here, but he's got nothing on me. I am much less worthy than he'll ever be." A couple of prayers later, another pastor said something like, "Lord, these men's sins put together don't come close to mine. I am nothing." And then it was my turn. I took a deep breath and began to pray: "Father, I thank you today that you have made me a saint. Thank you that you have made me worthy and that you have made me holy. I don't have to ask you to anoint me today because you have already anointed me with the blood of your Son. Please use us, your servants, today."

Maybe it sounds arrogant when you read it, but please know that wasn't my heart. That day, did I disagree with what my brothers were saying in their prayers? No. But I suggest we stop beating ourselves up in prayer. I understood the meaning behind each prayer offered that afternoon: In genuine humility, they were proclaiming to one another the truth that we all are failures without Jesus Christ. They were also confessing that although God had placed them in a position of influence, they were not without sin. They had a "be merciful to me, a sinner" heart (Luke 18:13), while in all sincerity, proclaiming their dependency on Jesus.

However, the declaration of our sinfulness must be balanced with the proclamation of our sainthood in Christ. In Romans 1:7, Paul refers to the believers in Rome as "those... called to be saints." We are sinners, but we are also saints. Yes, even with Christ in our lives, we lose some battles as we struggle with sin. But we will never lose the war. The worship band Starfield's song "Revolution," says it best: "I am a war already won." We have to humbly remind ourselves that we will lose many battles in life, yet still find our position as saints intact. If we continually harp on our failures, we will achieve a defeatist mentality. It's exhausting to live in perpetual defeat. It's liberating to leave behind the past and to grow in our new identity as saints. Our identity as believers is not lessened with each passing defeat but is sealed through Christ's revolution. I am not suggesting that we are to walk with a self-righteous stride, but with a confidence born from Christ's righteousness. We are not perfect, just forgiven. As believers, when God looks at us he sees the righteousness of Christ.

Satan desires to give us an identity crisis. He tries to make us forget who we are in Christ. When we are without Christ, Satan tells us that we are already saints. We're not that bad, and we don't need the grace of God to save us. But then when we become Christians, Satan changes his tune and keeps telling us that we are sinners and will never find victory from the bondage of sin. After all, Satan is the father of lies. Sadly, when we buy into his lies, we don't have an "I'm a war already won" confidence in our identity in Christ. Every time we sin, we think, *I'm going to sin because that's what I am, a sinner.* This is what Satan wants for all Christians: life in a constant identity crisis. He wants us full of spiritual defeat.

Remember my friend Jonah—the missionary whose real name is really not *Jonah*? Well, let me tell you something funny about him. Jonah grew up in China and in the Chinese culture. When he moved to Mississippi, he fell into an identity crisis. Everything about him began to change. He now speaks with a Southern drawl, wears wranglers and cowboy boots, drives a pick-up truck, and wants to marry a sweet Southern girl. Once, we asked Jonah what he wanted us to send him while he was out on the mission field. His reply was, "A can of chicken and dumplings!!" Who ever heard of an Asian person's favorite food being chicken and dumplings? I know that we kid him about it all the time because it's funny and harmless, but the illustration makes a good point. Jonah can talk, eat, and act like a guy from Mississippi, but he will always be Chinese.

Much like Jonah, we have an identity crisis in the church today. The people of God have lost track of their true identity in Christ. As Christians, when we sin, we are acting in contradiction to who we are. The next time you are tempted to sin, remind yourself that you are a saint. Instead of saying, *I can't help it, I'm just a sinner, say, I'm not going to act in contradiction to who I am! I'm a saint, I've been forgiven, and I have a new identity.*

In Ephesians 2:6, Paul says that we are raised up with him and seated with him in the heavenly places in Christ Jesus. To be "in" Christ is to no longer be "in" the grasp of sin (remember Day 6). It is Christ's righteousness that makes us saints. Not anything we have done. This allows us to be saints, yet still walk in humility. We've done nothing to earn it or deserve it, so we can't take credit for it. Sadly today, to declare our sainthood out loud is perceived as arrogant. The type of humility that does not acknowledge who we are in Christ, but makes us appear less than who we are, is a false humility. It downplays the amazing fact that Christ has imparted his righteousness to us. Paul explains this balance when he refers to himself in Ephesians 3:8 as "the very least of all the saints." Will we ever live a life of perfection simply by telling ourselves that we are saints? No, we won't achieve perfection until we get to heaven. But we can find ourselves more victorious in battles by recognizing that our righteousness and strength are forever found in God's grace. We can live as a war already won.

Be Still. Listen to what God is saying to you.

1. Although you might sin every day, as a Christian do you believe your identity is that of a saint? Why?

2. As a Christian, why is your position as a saint not determined by your feelings or your sinful actions?

3. As a saint, why do you still find yourself sinning? (Paul talks about this same struggle in Romans 7:15-25.)

4. Our sainthood should be humbling and not something to make us arrogant. Why? What do you think Paul means when he says: "I am the least of the saints"?

5. Write a sentence about how being "a war already won" applies to you.

Lord, I thank you that today your grace is *comforting* me in these areas:

Lord, I thank you that today your grace is *convicting* me in these areas:

Lord, I thank you that today your grace is *calling* me to:

Today's Memory Verses: Ephesians 2:1-8

Freedom

*"And you were dead in the trespasses and sins in which you once walked, following the prince of the power of the air, the spirit that is now at work in the sons of disobedience—among whom we all once lived in the passions of our flesh, carrying out the desires of the body and the mind, and were by nature children of wrath, like the rest of mankind. But God, being rich in mercy, because of the great love with which he loved us, even when we were dead in our trespasses, made us alive together with Christ—by grace you have been saved—**and raised us** up with him and seated us with him in the heavenly places in Christ Jesus, so that in the coming ages he might show the immeasurable riches of his grace in kindness toward us in Christ Jesus. For by grace you have been saved through faith. And this is not your own doing; it is the gift of God, not a result of works, so that no one may boast. For we are his workmanship, created in Christ Jesus for good works, which God prepared beforehand, that we should walk in them."*

(Ephesians 2:1-10)

If you were on a deserted island and only had ten DVDs to watch for the rest of your life, what would they be? Sure, there is no electricity on a deserted island, nor would there be a DVD player, so I'm guessing your answer would be, "Probably the ones that would taste the best." I suppose what I'm really asking is, "What are your favorite movies?" Yes, I realize that some of you are sitting in your room right now yelling, *"How Stella Got Her Groove Back!"* But for most of us the list usually contains epics that have stood the test of time. Look at most people's DVD collections, those they could not just rent but had to buy, and you will probably find among others, *The Shawshank Redemption*, *The Patriot*, and *Schindler's List*. Not too long ago, as I was straightening up my own DVDs, I noticed a common thread woven throughout most of the movies I own. From the ones I mentioned above to *The Matrix*, *Amistad*, and *The Green Mile*, the theme became evident: freedom. Can't you just see William Wallace in the movie *Braveheart* standing on the front line of the battle, yelling, "Freedom!"?

I believe the reason we are drawn to that theme is because we are all born with an insatiable desire for freedom. God created us with that desire. Why? God, himself, has that desire. As we look at what it means to be "raised up," one of the truths Paul refers to is the power of God's grace to raise us up from bondage to freedom. We are raised to be in the presence of the Lord, and there is no place more majestic and high. In 2 Corinthians 3:17, the Bible tells us that "the Lord is the Spirit, and where the Spirit of the Lord is, there is freedom." If we are in the presence of God (with him), our souls are completely free.

Paul is also referring to the truth that we are seated with Christ. When Christ was raised from the dead and seated at the Father's side (Ephesians 1:20), he took us with him. Spiritually speaking, we go from bondage in a prison, to freedom in a mansion. Wow! If that's not a "raise," then I don't know what is! Let's look at three statements about freedom that build on one another.

1. God is a free God.

In Psalm 115, the psalmist declares, "Our God is in the heavens; he does all that he pleases." We serve a God who has always been free to do whatever he wants as long as it is consistent with his holy character. God, the true leader of the free world does not rely on polls and surveys from us to make decisions. God is bound by nothing, including man, and always acts according to his own will. He does anything and everything that pleases himself in order to carry out his good purposes. When God is carrying out his decisions, he checks with no one to get approval. This is evident throughout both the Old and New Testaments. From Genesis to Revelation, we see a God who works freely. In practical application, this allows us to trust God even when we disagree with, or do not understand, what he is doing. By the way, this is the kind of God we want to serve—an all-powerful, all-knowing Father, who is not in a co-dependant relationship with us.

2. God is a free God who sets us free.

God in his own free will allows us to be set free through what Christ did for us on the cross. Through God's grace we are released from the chains of sin and legalism and are made free in Christ. Christ is the key that unlocks the chains. First, Jesus sets us free from the bondage of sin by paying the penalty for all our sins on the cross. This sets us free from our sinful nature. Second, he sets us free from legalism by giving us the ability to love him with our good works, not so that we can earn his favor, but because we already have his favor. In the words of Christ himself, "So if the Son sets you free, you will be free indeed" (John 8:36).

3. God is a free God who sets us free for freedom's sake.

In Galatians 5:1 where Paul says, "It is for freedom that Christ has set us free" (NIV), he might sound redundant at first glance, but he is making a strong and clear point about our freedom in Christ, and that is extremely important for us to grasp. What Paul is reminding us of is that God did not set the captives free so that we can hang out around the jail cell and live as though we are still prisoners. He is calling us to live the free life. Free from guilt. Free from addiction to worldly things. But most importantly, free from who we were. God did not set us free from sin to call us to a life of legalistic bondage; that would be taking us from one prison and putting us in another. Nor did he free us to live without boundaries. He has instead "raised us up" to a place where there is freedom. Freedom to worship the one, true God. Freedom to live a life of service and obedience. Freedom to love without limits. "Free at last, free at last, thank God almighty, I'm free at last..."

Oh, yeah. I forgot to mention one other movie that became an instant classic and a "must own" DVD. You might have heard of it—*The Passion of the Christ.* What was its central theme? Think about it. Freedom.

Be Still. Listen to what God is saying to you.

1. Define *freedom*.

2. Spiritually speaking, what does being free mean I should do?

   What does being free mean I should not do?

3. What is God's plan to set us free?

   Why does God set us free?

4. What does Paul mean when he says, "It is for freedom that Christ has set us free" (Galatians 5:1 NIV)?

Lord, I thank you that today your grace is *comforting* me in these areas:

Lord, I thank you that today your grace is *convicting* me in these areas:

Lord, I thank you that today your grace is *calling* me to:

Today's Memory Verses: Ephesians 2:1-8

Glory train

"And you were dead in the trespasses and sins in which you once walked, following the prince of the power of the air, the spirit that is now at work in the sons of disobedience—among whom we all once lived in the passions of our flesh, carrying out the desires of the body and the mind, and were by nature children of wrath, like the rest of mankind. But God, being rich in mercy, because of the great love with which he loved us, even when we were dead in our trespasses, made us alive together with Christ—by grace you have been saved—and raised us up with him and seated us with him in the heavenly places in Christ Jesus, ***so that in the coming ages he might show the immeasurable riches of his grace in kindness toward us in Christ Jesus.*** *For by grace you have been saved through faith. And this is not your own doing; it is the gift of God, not a result of works, so that no one may boast. For we are his workmanship, created in Christ Jesus for good works, which God prepared beforehand, that we should walk in them."*

(Ephesians 2:1-10)

Why did Jesus die on the cross? Why does God extend us grace when we deserve his wrath?

I've been asking these two questions a lot lately from the stage. Not just as rhetorical questions, but literally asking people from the audience to raise a hand if they want to give an answer. On average the number one answer is, "Because he loved us." Number two is, "So we can go to heaven." Number three is usually, "Because that's the only way we can be saved." I want to suggest to you that these answers are not wrong answers, but just not the main answer. It couldn't be truer that God loves us (John 3:16). It is also true that Jesus Christ is the only way to heaven (John 14:6). But in Ephesians 2:7-9, Paul makes it clear that God's ultimate intent in extending grace by saving us through his Son was that he might bring himself glory. Paul is saying that God wants to "show the immeasurable riches of his grace" so that no man can boast.

Expressed another way would be that God chose to bring himself glory by showing grace to undeserving me. Pastor Jonathan Edwards once said, "It is manifest from scripture that God's glory is the last end of...the work of redemption by Jesus Christ."[1] Our salvation is the benefit of grace, not the great intent. Jesus himself makes his ultimate purpose very clear when in John 12:27-28 he says in the Garden of Gethsemane, "Now is my soul troubled. And what shall I say? 'Father, save me from this hour?' But for this purpose I have come to this hour. Father, glorify your name."

Think about it: If God's ultimate purpose for Christ dying on the cross was so that we could be saved, then it's all about you and me. Right? However, Christ tells us that he came to the cross for the purpose of glorifying God by providing a way for us to be justified. God's ultimate purpose is *not* about me—it's about *him.* I am reminded of the opening line in Rick Warren's best-selling book *The Purpose Driven Life.*[2] The first line of chapter one reads, "It's not about you." Rick's entire book is all about aligning our purpose with God's great purpose. NOT THE PURPOSE OF ME, BUT THE PURPOSE OF THEE. It's amazing how man-centered the gospel has become to many people in the church today.

When the gospel is all about making much of us, then it becomes about our glory. The word *glory* means weight or heavy. To bring glory to God is to put much weight behind whom he is, or to not take *lightly* what he says. Have you ever heard someone say, "He took what I said lightly," or, "There wasn't much weight behind what he said"? Well, what is meant is that little importance or emphasis was given to the statement. See? To take God heavily or to make much of him, not little of him, is to give God glory.

God wants us to make him *heavy* in our lives. So heavy, in fact, that he becomes our lives. Simply put, he wants all the glory. "I am the Lord; that is my name; my glory I give to no other, nor my praise to carved idols" (Isaiah 42:8). Charles Spurgeon once said, "The great end of God in Christ was the manifestation of his own glorious attributes." Spurgeon is saying that God's glory is the revelation of his own character. In other words, when we seek the glory of God, we are seeking him. God's glory is not the light that shines around him; it *is* him.

By extending grace to ungracious me, the Lord shows the immeasurable riches of his grace in kindness toward us in Christ Jesus. Again, I don't deserve his mercy, so when I do receive it undeservingly, he becomes the center of all the attention and glory. This is why Jesus says about himself in John 7:18 that he "seeks the glory of him who sent him." Jesus was all about the glory of the Father. Guess what we should be all about?

Maybe you don't like what you're reading because you feel it's implying that God is boastful and a show-off. Well, God is a show-off. Don't worry! Lightning is not going to strike me down for writing it, nor you for reading it. If you read Ephesians 2:7-10, you'll see that Paul agrees. We live in a world today where the word show-off has a negative connotation. Let's face it—we usually don't like show-offs. They are always pointing out what they have done or where they have been, boasting in order to make much of themselves. It seems self-promoting. Showing off also implies that no one else is as good. Give me a show off, and I will give you someone obsessed with his own self. The fact is, it is wrong for you and me to be show-offs. It is the sin of pride. We would be bringing undue glory to ourselves.

So, all that said, why would it be OK and not irreverent to call God a show-off? The answer is simply this: with God, and only with God, to show off is appropriate and right. When you and I show off, we bring undue attention to ourselves. When God shows off, he brings due attention to himself.

In many ways, to show off is to worship or celebrate self. This act is not only inappropriate, but it is sin in our lives. It is arrogance. In Luke 18:14, Jesus says, "For everyone who exalts himself will be humbled, but the one who humbles himself will be exalted." Proverbs 11:2 also states, "When pride comes, then comes disgrace, but with the humble is wisdom." For God, however, the act of worshiping self is his ultimate and appropriate purpose. Think about it: God created us to worship him. You and I are supposed to worship and bring attention to God. But who does God worship? To whom should God bring attention? Could anyone or anything be any more worthy than God himself? A holy God finds ultimate pleasure in a perfectly holy being. Who is perfectly holy but God? It is only right and appropriate then that God find delight in himself first and foremost.

When God shows off his power through the ocean tide, or his gentle spirit through morning dew, he is doing exactly what God should be doing. He is bringing glory to himself, because there is no other greater than he. "The heavens declare the glory of God, and the sky above proclaims his handiwork" (Psalm 19:1). When we look at all the portraits of grace we've been reading over the past few weeks, who gets the ultimate glory for these lives that have overcome hard circumstances? The one who allowed them to overcome!

The very first of the Ten Commandments is, "Thou shalt have no other gods before me" (Exodus 20:3). Why? Because God wants to be the only one worshiped. Why does God want to be the only one worshiped? He wants all the glory.

Recently a friend of mine accused me of jumping on the "glory train." He said that he was tired of all the speakers who were jumping on the bandwagon of preaching about the topic of God's glory. He said, "A couple of years ago it was the worship fad, and now it's all glory this, glory that." The "glory of God" sermons were, in his opinion, the trendy new thing to preach. This was a minister talking!

I was so broken-hearted that a fellow co-laborer saw it as a "bandwagon" topic. I told him that it was not a new fad, but a topic that God has been recently rising up in the hearts of many preachers. Because we are all more self-centered than ever, we all need to hear God-centered preaching more than ever. This must start with the gospel and its ultimate purpose. I told my friend I saw it as an honor that God has allowed me to jump on his "glory train." To be on that train is to be in good company. I can just see Paul sticking his head out of the window of a steam engine, yelling, "Soli Deo Gloria [To God Alone Be the Glory]—all aboard the glory train!" Show off God.

Be Still. Listen to what the Lord is saying to you.

1. Define *glory*. What is the difference between man's glory and God's glory?

3. What was the ultimate purpose of Jesus' death?

4. Take a few moments and write down some things in your life that take glory from God.

5. List some of the ways in which God has shown himself off in your life (great "God memories").

Lord, I thank you that today your grace is *comforting* me in these areas:

Lord, I thank you that today your grace is *convicting* me in these areas:

Lord, I thank you that today your grace is *calling* me to:

Today's Memory Verses: Ephesians 2:1-8

In Life There Will Be Tears

Portrait of Grace

Did you know there is no age limit on a college application? Belle Patterson discovered this when applying to Shelton State Community College at the age of sixty alongside her daughter. Can you imagine graduating college with your mother beside you? Fulfilling her lifelong dream at the age of sixty plus was extraordinary. But then, nothing for Belle Patterson had ever happened on an ordinary timetable.

Mrs. Patterson was born a sharecropper's daughter in rural Alabama in 1920. Her dad was a godly man, who was an "old school" itinerant preacher. He would sometimes preach at a church and literally come home with a chicken as his pay. Mrs. Patterson shared the home with her mother and three brothers and sisters. Life was hard with no electricity or running water, but it was beautiful nonetheless. Like most girls, many of her childhood years were spent dreaming of marrying and starting a family. But as the years marched on, it seemed that day would never come. Eventually, all of her other brothers and sisters married and moved off. Mrs. Patterson chose to honor her now elderly parents by staying at home during the prime of her life to care for them. In her late thirties, marriage and children seemed like a faraway dream. "With my parents having gone on to be with the Lord, I was forty-one when God decided to bring home the love of my life. I didn't date around to find him. God brought him to me. The Lord's timing is always right," she says. Her husband, Rev. Ira Patterson, whom she lovingly continues to talk about to this day, was a preacher of the gospel. They had one daughter, Karen. Mrs. Patterson remembers her marriage to Rev. Patterson as the happiest time of her life. They enjoyed life with each other and always thought they would "finish the race" together. However, for Mrs. Patterson, God worked on his own timetable and his own plans.

Jennifer and I always thought that Rev. Patterson had a heart attack while preaching in the pulpit. Mrs. Patterson set us straight recently by telling us, "No, no, he had just finished the message. He had stepped down from the pulpit and was praying the benediction. I was only two or three rows back when it happened." She rushed to his side as he collapsed thinking, *I just can't believe he's gone. I've only had eight short years with him. What am I going to do now?* He died the following Tuesday, and the next day around two in the morning, she found herself sobbing. She prayed, "Lord, what am I going to do now?" The Lord replied, "There's a car out there in that driveway—learn to drive it." And she obeyed. At the age of fifty, this fiery redhead learned to drive a car, raise a daughter, teach Sunday school...and eventually graduate from college.

If you ask her how she did it, she will say one thing—"the grace of God." He alone has sustained her, counseled her, comforted her, and protected her. Mrs. Patterson speaks continually about the goodness of God in her life and his faithfulness to her. She is my wife's mentor and a great-grandmother to our children. Today, living on a tiny budget in government housing, Mrs. Belle Patterson is one of the richest people we know. She never fails to have several Bible verses on the tip of her tongue (references included). She has lost count of the times she has read the Bible completely through, and is continually looking for ways she can serve and evangelize. Jennifer recently asked her permission to tell her story in this book. She humbly accepted, and when asked to sum up what God has taught her through all the years of good and bad in her life, Mrs. Patterson said the following: "In life, there will be tears, but don't sit down to cry. You can cry, but keep going. Do something while you're crying. God might ask you to do something that is scary to you, but, honey, you can trust him."

For Belle Kizziah Patterson, God's grace truly is sufficient.

Grace Extension

Mrs. Belle Patterson has been extending grace to my wife for as long as I have known Jennifer. Jennifer can specifically recall so many different times in her life that she went to Mrs. Patterson's home with the intent to be a blessing, but ended up being the one blessed. This is usually the case when you reach out to the elderly. Whether it's wisdom from the past, perspective for the future, or simply a listening ear, elderly people have a lot to give. Today's Grace Extension is an opportunity to be a blessing to a lonely saint.

Here are some suggestions. Most are pretty obvious, but all are about building a relationship:

Cook or buy a meal and deliver it. (Check dietary restrictions first.)

Take flowers and a hand-written card.

Rake leaves, plant flowers, or do other yard work.

Clean the house or at least a closet.

Offer to organize old photos into an album.

Visit a nursing home and read for an elderly person with bad eyesight.

Organize a Christmas gift drive for your local nursing home.

Again, outside of the obvious physical benefits of these acts of service, there is the life-changing opportunity for a senior in high school to develop a relationship with a senior citizen! For example, when organizing a photo album—as you help, allow the senior adult to tell the stories behind each pictures. More than an album is being developed—a relationship is being established. Contact any local church or nursing home and there will be no problem finding a person with whom to connect.

Be Involved!

Today's Memory Verses: Ephesians 2:1-9

Lord, I thank you that today your grace is *comforting* me in these areas:

Lord, I thank you that today your grace is *convicting* me in these areas:

Lord, I thank you that today your grace is *calling* me to:

Today's Memory Verses: Ephesians 2:1-9

Faith

"And you were dead in the trespasses and sins in which you once walked, following the prince of the power of the air, the spirit that is now at work in the sons of disobedience—among whom we all once lived in the passions of our flesh, carrying out the desires of the body and the mind, and were by nature children of wrath, like the rest of mankind. But God, being rich in mercy, because of the great love with which he loved us, even when we were dead in our trespasses, made us alive together with Christ—by grace you have been saved—and raised us up with him and seated us with him in the heavenly places in Christ Jesus, so that in the coming ages he might show the immeasurable riches of his grace in kindness toward us in Christ Jesus. ***For by grace you have been saved through faith.*** *And this is not your own doing; it is the gift of God, not a result of works, so that no one may boast. For we are his workmanship, created in Christ Jesus for good works, which God prepared beforehand, that we should walk in them."*

(Ephesians 2:1-10)

I was in a Circuit City a few months ago looking for a TV. I told the salesman that I needed an unbelievable deal—one that couldn't be passed up. I was on a hunt for an old display model, or even a returned one that they had to get rid of. "This is your lucky day—have I got a deal for you!" he informed me as we walked to the back of the store. There, in all its glory, sat every man's best friend: fifty-four inches of flat-screened plasma satisfaction! Oh yeahhh! The salesman continued, explaining that this set was a floor-model display and that there were a few things missing. And if I could live without a few parts here and there, I could own an amazing TV for about 75 percent off!

Here's what was missing:

No box—no problem

No owner's manual—no problem

No remote—no problem

No power cord—BIG PROBLEM

The salesman further explained that the reason the TV was such a good deal was because it had a special power cord that couldn't be replaced. Another company bought out the company that had manufactured the TV, and production of that particular power cord was discontinued.

"The problem is this TV needs power. Without a cord, how do I connect it to the power?" I asked.

"Well, that is a problem, isn't it?" But he

exclaimed, "That's why it's such a good deal!"

No matter how expensive the TV or how incredible the deal; it is worthless if there is no way to connect to its source of power.

In Ephesians 2:8, Paul is teaching us that faith is very similar to this power cord. Obviously, Paul didn't have a TV back then, but please indulge me for the sake of this illustration: just as a TV needs a power cord to connect it with the source of electricity needed to turn it on and keep it on; we, as Christians, need *faith* to allow *grace* to turn us on and keep us on. God's *grace* is the power, and *faith* is the extension cord that plugs us into this power. Pastor Tony Evans writes, "Faith is the wire over which the current of God's grace travels to bring you the privileges of your identity in Christ...We could say that grace gives you what you have; faith enables you to experience what grace gives you."[1] Faith allows us to access the power of grace. Just as a TV cannot access the electricity it needs in order to operate without a cord, we cannot access the grace we need to operate without faith.

Look at Paul's words "For by grace you have been saved through faith." Now, let's connect that to the TV illustration. "For by electricity you have been turned on through the cord." Do you see it? This is saving faith—a faith that takes us from off to on. This shows us that ultimately it is the source of power that deserves the credit, not the cord itself. The cord simply accesses the power. Our faith should not get the credit for our salvation, but God's grace should. Charles Spurgeon once wrote, "Our life is found in 'looking unto Jesus,' not in looking to our own faith. By faith all things become possible to us; yet the power is not in the faith, but in the God upon whom faith relies."[2]

Another fact about the power cord is that not only is the cord needed to turn the TV on; it is needed to keep the TV on. The same is true about faith. As Christians, we must recognize that not only are we saved by grace through faith, but we are also sustained by grace through faith. This is sustaining faith—a faith that keeps us on. What keeps us on is not the cord itself (faith), but the power that flows through the cord (grace). There's a declaration of sustaining faith that Jennifer learned at a Beth Moore Bible study:

God is who he says he is.
God can do what he says he can do.
I am who God says I am.
I can do all things through Christ.
God's Word is alive and active in me.
I'm believing God!

What an incredible statement! Even as you were reading it, couldn't you just feel God's current of sustaining grace flowing through you? That, my friend, is one great deal!

Be Still. Listen to what God is saying to you.

1. In the opening illustration, what created the problem with the TV? How is this a parallel to the Christian life?

2. Like the extension cord to the TV, faith allows us to...(finish the sentence and expand).

3. What is the difference between *saving faith* and *sustaining faith*?

4. List enemies of faith (fear, doubt, etc.) and describe your struggles with them.

Lord, I thank you that today your grace is *comforting* me in these areas:

Lord, I thank you that today your grace is *convicting* me in these areas:

Lord, I thank you that today your grace is *calling* me to:

Today's Memory Verses: Ephesians 2:1-9

Free gift

"And you were dead in the trespasses and sins in which you once walked, following the prince of the power of the air, the spirit that is now at work in the sons of disobedience—among whom we all once lived in the passions of our flesh, carrying out the desires of the body and the mind, and were by nature children of wrath, like the rest of mankind. But God, being rich in mercy, because of the great love with which he loved us, even when we were dead in our trespasses, made us alive together with Christ—by grace you have been saved—and raised us up with him and seated us with him in the heavenly places in Christ Jesus, so that in the coming ages he might show the immeasurable riches of his grace in kindness toward us in Christ Jesus. For by grace you have been saved through faith. ***And this is not your own doing; it is the gift of God, not a result of works, so that no one may boast.*** *For we are his workmanship, created in Christ Jesus for good works, which God prepared beforehand, that we should walk in them."*

(Ephesians 2:1-10)

The Texas Cadillac. Now if you're a Texan, those words warrant no explanation. For those of you who are not, I'm talking about the gas guzzlin', "W" bumpersticker wearin', ozone-layer killin' Chevy Suburban. Coming in at an eco-friendly nine miles to the gallon, the Suburban is driven not only by ranchers and soccer moms but also by evangelists who have to lug their families and their luggage from one ministry opportunity to another. A few years ago, I was driving into a campsite when I saw a speaker friend of mine sporting a brand-new, candy-apple-red Suburban. I was on my way in; he was on his way out. We stopped at the gate and began to talk. I have to admit that I don't remember much of what he said for the first minute, because in the back of my mind all I kept thinking was, *I know this guy. He's a young minister, just starting out. He's usually way too broke to even rent a truck like this, much less buy one.* So I nonchalantly asked, "Hey, what's with the Suburban? Is this a loaner?" Brad then told me this unbelievable story:

"Dave, man, you're not going to believe this. All this week at camp we saw God do the most amazing things! Every night God did stuff that was so 'God-sized'! On the last night of camp, I decided to preach early in the service and let the worship follow me. As soon as I finished preaching, I stepped off the stage, stood in the front row, and began to worship along with the students. While I was singing, I felt a tap on my shoulder. Looking up I saw this big, intimidating guy who said, 'I want to talk with you right now. Outside!' The first thing that came to my mind was, *Oh, no! I've done something wrong and I'm about to get jumped.* But he was so big; I was not about to disobey him.

"I followed him out, all the way to the parking lot. That's when it happened. This guy looked me straight in the eyes and said, 'God told me to give you this. It's a gift.' He then reached in his pocket and pulled out a set of keys with a car-alarm key chain. He pointed to the parking lot and said, 'Go on out there. It's yours.' I have to admit that my first thought was, *Oh, no, Lord, please don't let it be a church van.* But seriously, when I pushed the button and I saw the lights flash on a brand-new, loaded Texas Cadillac, I was blown away. This guy just gave me his car. It's worth at least forty grand. Dave, can you believe it?"

I mumbled, "Uh, no." Then I replied, "Let me get this straight. That guy just gave you this car? So, what's the catch?"

Brad smiled, shook his head, and said, "I kept asking him the same question, but he kept telling me there was no catch. It's just a gift."

I was so excited for him. We both started to rejoice together.

"Brad, this is too good to be true."

I will never forget his response. "David, I know it's too good to be true! But it's too good, *and* it's true!"

Those words have stuck with me ever since. They contain the powerful truth of something far greater than anything this world has to offer. These words represent an essential foundation of the grace of God. If truth were told, God's grace is a free gift that sounds way too good to be true, but it's too good *and* it's true. Obviously, the gift of grace is far superior to a free car, but for the sake of illustration, let's look at some parallels between Brad's Texas Cadillac and the free gift of salvation.

Uno – Brad received a gift he did not have the ability to pay for himself. When we receive the grace of God, we receive a gift we could never have earned ourselves due to our sinful state.

Dos – Brad's gift was free to Brad, but not free. The one who could afford to pay for it had paid for it. This, Brad knew, did not make the gift cheap and worthless just because he had received it free. The gift of salvation is also free to us, but bare in mind it is *not* free. Jesus was the only one who could pay the complete debt for our sins.

Tres – The last thing Brad needed to think was, *Since it didn't cost me anything, I won't put any effort whatsoever into taking care of this car. I won't ever change the oil, check the filters, or do anything to keep the car in good shape. As a matter of fact, I think I'll just crash it into a wall. What do I care? It didn't cost me anything.*

Not only would this eventually make the car incapable of running to its full potential, at the very least this would completely dishonor the one who gave him the car.

Likewise, when you and I receive the free gift of salvation, the last thing we should think is, *Well, I guess since it didn't cost me anything, I am not responsible to grow in my walk with God and to live in a victorious relationship with him. I won't ever go to church, read my Bible, pray, or do anything spiritual. As a matter of fact, let me see what kind of sins I can get away with!*

Not only will this result in a wayward life, at the very least it would dishonor the one who saved us by his loving grace. Grace doesn't give us the license to sin, but the freedom not to.

Quatro – The primary focus of the Suburban story isn't Brad, or even the Suburban. The attention rightfully is placed on the amazing kindness of the giver. We, then, should recognize that the true giver is God who chose to use this selfless servant to ultimately deliver this generous gift to Brad.

The true grace message doesn't place the attention to us, the receiver, but on the amazing love of God, the giver. God, in his kindness, ultimately used Jesus to deliver his generous gift of salvation to us. Pastor John Piper, in his book *The Godward Life*, writes about trying to turn God's grace into a business transaction by attempting to somehow pay him back. This nullifies the grace of God, and "God does not like to have His grace nullified. He likes to have it glorified" (Ephesians 1: 6, 12, 14).[1]

Paul shouts this truth to us in Ephesians 2:8-9 when he says, "And this is not your own doing; it is the gift of God, not a result of works, so that no one may boast."

He is saying that you and I simply need to receive the free gift of grace. We can't do anything to earn salvation. It is a free gift; therefore, we won't receive any attention and boast. God alone gets the glory. In Charles Swindoll's book *The Grace Awakening*, this truth is shared as well: "Everyone who hopes to be eternally justified must come to God the same way: on the basis of grace; it is a gift. And that gift comes to us absolutely free. Any other view of salvation is heresy, plain and simple."[2]

Grace sounds too good to be true—it is too good, and it is true.

Not just a gift, but also the greatest gift of all.

Be Still. Listen to what God is saying to you.

1. If someone gave you an unbelievable gift, like a free car, and said no strings attached, whatsoever, what would be your reaction? Is this reaction similar or different to how you react to God's grace?

2. If we could pay God back, what would grace become?

3. Why does God not want a payment? What is his intent behind making the gift of salvation free?

4. How do we dishonor God's free gift of grace? How should we honor God's free gift of grace?

Lord, I thank you that today your grace is *comforting* me in these areas:

Lord, I thank you that today your grace is *convicting* me in these areas:

Lord, I thank you that today your grace is *calling* me to:

Today's Memory Verses: Ephesians 2:1-9

Masterpiece

"And you were dead in the trespasses and sins in which you once walked, following the prince of the power of the air, the spirit that is now at work in the sons of disobedience—among whom we all once lived in the passions of our flesh, carrying out the desires of the body and the mind, and were by nature children of wrath, like the rest of mankind. But God, being rich in mercy, because of the great love with which he loved us, even when we were dead in our trespasses, made us alive together with Christ—by grace you have been saved—and raised us up with him and seated us with him in the heavenly places in Christ Jesus, so that in the coming ages he might show the immeasurable riches of his grace in kindness toward us in Christ Jesus. For by grace you have been saved through faith. And this is not your own doing; it is the gift of God, not a result of works, so that no one may boast. ***For we are his workmanship, created in Christ Jesus*** *for good works, which God prepared beforehand, that we should walk in them."*
(Ephesians 2:1-10)

What makes a masterpiece a true masterpiece? The difference between a watercolor created by a high school art teacher and a painting by Picasso is more than just appearance. The difference between Beethoven's Fifth and some garage band's love sonnet about their school's cutest cheerleader is more than just the beat. What sets one masterpiece apart from another is the *master* who created it. Elvis Presley sings, "You ain't nothin' but a hound dog," and it's worth millions. If I wrote a song calling someone a four-legged animal, it would not only be worthless, but it would most likely get sued by an animal rights activist group claiming I hurt Fluffy's feelings.

Another characteristic of a true masterpiece is that it must be authentic. For example, my dad has a painting of the *Mona Lisa* in his French restaurant. With its ornate gold frame and museum-quality lighting, it looks both intimidating and expensive. However, it's obviously not the real thing. It never ceases to amaze me, though, how once in a while a redneck will wander in and sincerely ask, "Is that the real *Mona Lisa*?" I always want to say, "Yeah, Jethro, the real *Mona Lisa* is hanging in a restaurant in Birmingham, Alabama." But I don't, because, hey, what would Jesus do? Anyway, the difference between the real *Mona Lisa* and the fake one at my dad's place is that one is a duplicate, and the other is an original painted by master painter Leonardo da Vinci.

So having established that a true masterpiece is an authentic creation by a master creator, we're brought face to face with the truth that Paul claims in Ephesians 2:10: "For we are his workmanship, created in Christ Jesus." The word *workmanship* is another way of saying masterpiece. In essence, Paul is describing the transformation Christians experience, from worthless junk (when we are in Adam) to authentic beautiful pieces of art (created in Christ Jesus). Paul continues this thought in 1 Corinthians 15:49: "Just as we have borne the image of the man of dust [Adam], we shall also bear the image of the man of heaven [Jesus]." Therefore, verse ten of Ephesians chapter two is the outcome of verses 1-9. Let's quickly review: When we are in Adam, we are dead because of our sinful nature—a true tragedy. But through grace, by faith in Christ Jesus, we become masterpieces—a true portrait of grace.

Think about it. As Christians we all have the same Master. But we are not duplicates of one another. God makes each one of us different, unique, and one-of-a-kind; yet, at the same time we all bear the image of his Son. No one else is like you. Some of us were created as vibrant, loud colors that scream out the power of our God. Some were created as pastel colors, with gentle brush strokes showing the tender side of the heavenly artist. Some are abstract pieces of art (that would be me!!), some realistic; yet, we're all created by the Master's hand. God is the Master Creator who is unimaginably creative.

Although we as Christians are all created to be different, our common denominator is that we bear the same signature. Just like the *Mona Lisa* and *The Last Supper* are different masterpieces, they were each created by the same artist and bear the same signature; we are all created by God and bear the signature of Christ. I am Christ's *David Nasser*, and that's where my value lies. Our common trait as believers is that God created us, and the blood of Jesus has been used to sign the canvas of our lives.

If you've ever bought an original Thomas Kincade painting, its authenticity can be validated by examining the signature. Not just by the appearance of the signature, but by the ink. Thomas Kincade signs all of his masterpieces with a pen filled with a special ink mixed with a few drops of his very own blood. His signature contains his very own DNA. If a Thomas Kincade painting ever needs to be authenticated, have the signature examined. *The proof is in the blood!*

The same is true when it comes to us as believers. When our lives are signed and sealed by the blood of Jesus, it is his signature upon us that makes our faith authentic. If your Christianity is authentic, *the proof is in his blood.* "Knowing that you were ransomed from the futile ways inherited from your forefathers, not with perishable things such as silver or gold, but with the precious blood of Christ, like that of a lamb without blemish or spot"

(1 Peter 1:18-19). Even if the paint is running and the frame is all bent out of shape, as long as the signature is authentic, you are still a masterpiece. However, if you feel more like a *mess-terpiece* than a *masterpiece*, then know that the Master is not finished. He loves you just the way you are, but he loves you too much to leave you that way.

In the museum of life, God has created you and me as pieces of art. When others see the masterpieces we have become in Christ (signed by his blood), we bring fame to the Master. That is the purpose of a masterpiece. "For by him all things were created, in heaven and on earth, visible and invisible, whether thrones or dominions or rulers or authorities—all things were created *through* him and *for* him" (Colossians 1:16 emphasis added).

In the midst of all the wreckage caused by the years of bombing during World War II, there was a man who vowed to eventually create a masterpiece out of all the devastation surrounding him. U.S. Army chaplain Fredrick Alexander McDonald drove many miles through the war-torn countries in Europe, offering prayer and counsel to soldiers marching into Germany. During his travels, he would go to the bombed-out remains of churches and cathedrals and collect pieces of the once-beautiful stained-glass windows that had been destroyed. McDonald carefully saved these shards of glass, hoping one day that they could be made into a memorial to those who suffered and served during those horrible years. Today, the legacy of his dream remains. Those pieces are now in the process of being crafted into two-dozen stained-glass windows, each etched with the stories of those who sacrificed so much. They are specifically designed to cast sacred light into houses of worship. What a beautiful parallel of how God designs and creates our lives. God is the Master Craftsman who specializes in taking the shattered remains of any life and working them into an artistic masterpiece through which the light of his grace can shine.

Be Still. Listen to what God is saying to you.

1. What is a masterpiece? What makes a work of art a masterpiece?

2. Spiritually speaking, what makes us go from worthless tragedies to worthy masterpieces?

3. What do all Christians have in common as masterpieces?

4. In the McDonald window illustration, we see how God takes the broken pieces and makes a beautiful masterpiece for his glory. How has this been true in your life?

Lord, I thank you that today your grace is *comforting* me in these areas:

Lord, I thank you that today your grace is *convicting* me in these areas:

Lord, I thank you that today your grace is *calling* me to:

Today's Memory Verses: Ephesians 2:1-9

Stained-Glass Lives

Shattered glass. Just saying those words makes one cringe a little. It brings up an image of an object that has been broken beyond repair. If you have ever been cut by pieces of broken glass, there may also be memories of pain involved in those words. As discussed yesterday, the great thing about shattered glass is that, although it can no longer be the object it once was, it can be salvaged to form a new object—stained glass. All have seen beautiful picture windows, in a church or cathedral somewhere, that were uniquely made from thousands of small pieces of glass. You cannot fully appreciate how amazing these works of art are until the sunlight shines through...

Dale and Jena Forehand began married life with hope and promise. Raised in Christian homes, they were both believers. Dale was a deacon in their church; Jena was active in the music ministry; and they both taught the young married Sunday school class. Everything appeared picture perfect on the outside. But inside the marriage, everything was falling apart. Dale and Jena were shattering each other with anger and struggling for control. They expressed the frustrations of their unmet needs not only on each other but on their two children, Cole and Jorga, as well. Things eventually escalated to the point when one day Dale packed their bags and drove off with the children, leaving Jena sobbing in the driveway.

Over the next few months, the situation grew only worse. Both Dale and Jena did everything they could to make things difficult on the other. The fighting reached a new level of viciousness, when Dale and his brother physically grabbed the children out of Jena's arms and took them to an unknown location for a week, resulting in Jena calling the police. Jena immediately filed for divorce, and because they both refused to leave the house or give up the children, the judge forced them to stay under the same roof for the fifteen-month-long divorce process. Dale and Jena both agreed it felt like prison. Their home continued to be a war zone:

they attended separate churches, and their families took sides. Nobody was surprised when the marriage ended in divorce. Sadly, over half of all marriages in America today end in divorce. Even sadder is the fact that statistics for Christian marriages are no different.

Four weeks after the divorce, in the middle of an argument, Jena surprised herself by revealing her vulnerability to Dale. Jena pleaded, "Dale, what have we done? Why don't you come get me? Let's fix this thing." Even more surprising than Jena's realization was Dale's quick response. "I can't even look at the feet of our children without seeing you." Evidence of the Holy Spirit at work! Jena recalls that Dale's statement was a bouquet of roses to her. God used that moment to shatter the hardness that had invaded both of their spirits. By the end of the conversation, they were both crying uncontrollably and pouring out their hearts to each other. Knowing that they had hurt each other so severely, they realized the road to restoration would take a lot of prayer, trust, and hard work. The Forehands spent the next four months in intense, God-centered marriage counseling. Through prayer and hard work the broken shards of their relationship were pieced back together with God's grace.

On December 21, 1997, Dale and Jena were remarried to the glory of God. They took the stone out of Jena's original ring and had it placed in a new setting to remind them of how God in his grace takes the old and makes it new again. God used the restoration of Dale and Jena's marriage in their son's life as well. Cole gave his life to the Lord on the morning of their remarriage. What a wedding present! Since then, God has used their story to show off his glory and grace, and he has allowed them to minister to thousands of people whose marriages are on the verge of total ruin. The Forehand family is a beautiful portrait of the healing grace of God.

No portrait is without its flaws. If you look at the lives of many saints in the Bible, you will see a continuous testimony of mistakes, failures, miscommunications, and wrongs done. You will also see a graceful God who consistently takes demolished lives and restores them into beautiful masterpieces. He does not return them to their original form, but renovates them, using all the shattered remains to form a completely new and unique construction. When reflecting on the twists and turns his life had taken, Joseph humbly said to his brothers in Genesis 50:20, "As for you, you meant evil against me, but God meant it for good, to bring it about that many people should be kept alive, as they are today." Think about it.

Grace Extension

There are times in everyone's life when the mountain seems formidable. We have faced these moments and thought, *How am I going to get through this?* In those times, a friendly "grace extension" can be a light at the end of the tunnel. When Dale and Jena Forehand were in the midst of their divorce, one thing they both realized was that their church families reached out to them. Think about it. To reach out is to extend. Today's Grace Extension is a call to reach out and minister to the hurting. Whether it's divorce, temptation, depression, or even the loss of a loved one, there are people all around us who are going through a really tough time. Here are some ideas of how to reach out:

1. Baby-sit for a single parent or a lady who needs to visit her sick mother in the hospital. Help lighten their load.

2. Send a card with an encouraging scripture to someone who is struggling. The Word of God is full of healing truth.

3. Think of someone who is hurting during the holidays and visit them or invite them over for dinner.

4. For a girl, send flowers. Never underestimate the power of a dozen roses. For a guy, send power tools! Never underestimate the power of a gift. We all love to receive something in the mail. It reminds us that someone is thinking of us and that we're not alone.

5. Most of the time, hurting people just need someone to listen. That may be why God gave us two ears and only one mouth, so we can listen twice as much as we speak. Go and be the kind of friend who will sit there and listen for as long as it takes. Sometimes we don't need to help fix things; we just need to listen.

6. There are times in life when the most helpful thing to do for someone is to recognize that you cannot help him or her by yourself. In severe circumstances, God might be using you to convince a friend to get professional Christian counseling or therapy. This is a tough one, because most of the time he doesn't feel as if he needs it. In this circumstance, you can recruit the help of your pastor. With his assistance, there can be an intervention moment, where your hurting friend can see the need for professional help.

7. You might have heard of "tough love." Well, this last extension is all about "tough extension." In rare occasions, the most graceful thing you can do is to stand against something destructively sinful that a friend is doing, and to lovingly say, "No more. Not on my watch!" The misconception about grace is that it must be passive. Don't be afraid to confront a friend who is hurting his own self or others. Our job is not to judge, but to hold them accountable. Accountability is a key part of any "grace extension."

Be Involved!

Today's Memory Verses: Ephesians 2:1-10

Lord, I thank you that today your grace is *comforting* me in these areas:

Lord, I thank you that today your grace is *convicting* me in these areas:

Lord, I thank you that today your grace is *calling* me to:

Today's Memory Verses: Ephesians 2:1-10

Grace & truth

"And you were dead in the trespasses and sins in which you once walked, following the prince of the power of the air, the spirit that is now at work in the sons of disobedience—among whom we all once lived in the passions of our flesh, carrying out the desires of the body and the mind, and were by nature children of wrath, like the rest of mankind. But God, being rich in mercy, because of the great love with which he loved us, even when we were dead in our trespasses, made us alive together with Christ—by grace you have been saved—and raised us up with him and seated us with him in the heavenly places in Christ Jesus, so that in the coming ages he might show the immeasurable riches of his grace in kindness toward us in Christ Jesus. For by grace you have been saved through faith. And this is not your own doing; it is the gift of God, not a result of works, so that no one may boast. ***For we are his workmanship, created in Christ Jesus for good works, which God prepared beforehand, that we should walk in them."***

(Ephesians 2:1-10)

A few years ago I was the speaker at an event in the Seattle area. On the second night of the three-day event, I decided to preach about the unchanging love of God. I set the backdrop for God's consistent love by discussing God's consistent nature. "For I the LORD, do not change" (Malachi 3:6). I spoke about how we change because we get new information, new revelation, etc., but God never changes. What God is against, he has always been against, and what he is for, he has always been for. God is not in heaven having an identity crisis, thinking, *Oh no, I have to reinvent myself so more people will love me. I guess what used to be wrong can now be OK, since I want to be more popular!*

To make my point, I went to Romans chapter one and shared the things Paul said God hated. The audience needed to understand that God is still against the same things he has always been against. He is eternally consistent, and his holy standard never changes. God is the same God today who showed his forgiveness and grace to his people during the Old Testament times. The intended message was God never changes..."God hates sin, but loves the sinner."

However, as I began reading Romans one, something very interesting happened. When I got to verses 26-27, several youth pastors stood and lead their entire youth group out of the room as a public act of disagreement. These men and women had serious issues with the scripture. Romans 1 states that God hates homosexuality among many other sins. Apparently these ministers felt that although God may be against the other sins in the list (such as envy, murder, boasting, and deceit), he has changed his mind on how he feels about homosexuality. In some of their churches, it is fine to live in a lifestyle of homosexual behavior because they believe that a loving God would never condemn someone for their sexual preference. After all, "God made us that way," one of the youth pastors told me later that night. My purpose in the message was to proclaim that God loves us (all of us—the homosexual, the murderer, the lustful, the legalist, etc.), but that he has a holy standard and cannot tolerate our sinful behavior. But to these men and women, they equated hating the sin with hating the sinner. Later on, after several hours of conversation with a large group of irritated people, I found myself being called a legalist, a hateful bigot, and even a heretic. Many of them said that I was not graceful. These men and women felt that I was not preaching the love of God, but that I was just passing judgment on behavior I didn't agree with.

The message that night was not exclusively about homosexuality, but to them it was. Homosexuality is not a biblically silent argument. God has spoken very clearly about homosexual behavior, and we should not have the luxury of picking which sins in scripture we agree with and which we want to ignore.

I never grew angry or quarrelsome that night. I truly believed that the most loving and graceful thing I could do was to preach the truth. After all, scripture calls me to gracefully preach the truth. Second Timothy 4:2-5 challenges, "Preach the word; be ready in season and out of season; reprove, rebuke, and exhort, with complete patience and teaching. For the time is coming when people will not endure sound teaching, but having itching ears they will accumulate for themselves teachers to suit their own passions, and will turn away from listening to the truth and wander off into myths. As for you, always be sober-minded, endure suffering, do the work of an evangelist, fulfill your ministry."

At the end of the day, these people wanted grace without truth. The Jesus they worshiped was one who was full of grace (I love you the way that you are), but not full of truth (I love you too much to leave you like this). The real Jesus is both grace and truth. Not a Jesus who is 50 percent grace and 50 percent truth, but a Jesus who is 100 percent grace and 100 percent truth. Look at what John 1:14 says about Christ: "And the Word became flesh and dwelt among us, and we have seen his glory, glory as of the only Son from the Father, full of grace and truth." John 1:17 reads, "For the law was given through Moses; grace and truth came through Jesus Christ."

Truth is something that is a fact and reality; the revelation of things as they actually exist. The Bible defines truth in several ways. One definition of truth is Jesus himself (John 14:6). Another definition of truth is the Word of God (John 17:17). Truth is also defined as God's holy standard. God sets his standard as the track for victorious living. Grace gets us on track (through saving faith), and keeps us on track (through sustaining faith), but grace does not give us permission to get off the track of truth. The term symbolically used here is *train wreck*. Our lives become a train wreck when we decide to get off the track and live by our own standard. That night in Seattle, there were people there who wanted to disregard God's standard about homosexuality and replace the holy standard of God with their own. Grace never replaces God's standard; it fulfills God's requirement and enables God's standard to be lived out through our lives.

On one side is the danger of legalism; on the other is the danger of liberalism. Grace without truth can lead to liberalism. Truth without grace can lead to legalism. The authentic grace-filled life is about both truth and grace being in union in us. Like two wings on a bird, both are essential. Randy Alcorn writes, "We should never approach truth except in a spirit of grace, or grace except in a spirit of truth."[1]

Take this test:

Have you ever thought, *I have got to start praying more, giving to the poor, and "living right" for God since I'm about to ask him for something. I need to get in his "good graces."*? If we think this way, we are leaning on the legalistic side. In this case, we need to repent of our self-righteousness.

Have you ever thought, *I'm going to go ahead and commit this sin since God will forgive me anyway. After all, it's for these moments that I have grace, right?* If we think this way, we are leaning on the liberal side. In this case we need to repent of our *un*righteousness.

Have you ever thought, *What should I do? Sin, so that grace might increase? No way! I have died to sin, so how can I live in this old life any longer?* (Romans 6:1). If you think this way, then you are balanced in both truth and grace. This is walking in *Christ's righteousness*.

In Ephesians 2:10, when Paul calls us to work, he is calling us to allow God, in grace and truth, to work through us. Paul was once a legalist himself, and he knew the dangers of walking in grace and truth among the extremely legalistic and the extremely permissive people of his day. Paul's convictions concerning grace and truth eventually cost him his life.

One of the first books I read when I first became a believer was *The Lion, the Witch, and the Wardrobe*. C. S. Lewis's classic is the story of four children who magically pass through the door of a wardrobe to find the magical kingdom of Narnia. Aslan, a massive lion, rules

Narnia. In this allegory, Aslan represents Christ. One of the children, Susan, asks Mr. Beaver, who lives in the forest, about Aslan. Mr. Beaver, who is loyal to Aslan, comforts Susan and the other children by telling them about Aslan. At one point Susan asks if Aslan is safe. Mr. Beaver replies, "Who said anything about safe? 'Course he isn't safe. But he's good. He's the King I tell you."[2] Wow, this is a powerful truth about Jesus. What a powerful allegory about grace and truth. Grace is not safe, but it is always good.

We often equate the word *good* with the word *nice*. *Good* does not necessarily mean *nice*. Many of the things Jesus said concerning the Pharisees and concerning hell would not be considered nice. However, Jesus always told the truth in a spirit of grace. We have all too often confused grace with passivity, avoidance, or indifference. Grace is not passive, avoiding of confrontation, nor indifferent. Grace is what it is. It is holy and truthful. Truth gives us convictions and the courage to confront, while grace allows us to speak these convictions with consideration and tact. I can confront my fellow believer about the blatant sin in his life using the authority of scripture (truth), but I can do it with a sense of compassion, not condemnation (grace). I can also live in a world among unbelievers and extend grace to them, but not conform to their beliefs. As Christians, although we must lovingly live among people we don't agree with, this is not an excuse to compromise our own convictions (John 17:15-17).

Jesus Christ is our supreme example of how someone can operate in a grace-and-truth mentality. He was and is never legalistic and never liberal. He never compromised the standard, yet he never acted in a spirit of condemnation. What a lesson for all believers.

Be Still. Listen to what God is saying to you.

1. What is truth? What is grace?

2. Why is it unloving not to tell someone the truth?

3. Has there ever been a time when someone confronted you in grace, and you were mad at him or her for doing it? Did you know deep down that they were right?

4. What are some things you do that could be considered legalistic? What are some things you do that could be considered liberal? How can you find a balance?

Lord, I thank you that today your grace is *comforting* me in these areas:

Lord, I thank you that today your grace is *convicting* me in these areas:

Lord, I thank you that today your grace is *calling* me to:

Today's Memory Verses: Ephesians 2:1-10

Responsibility

"And you were dead in the trespasses and sins in which you once walked, following the prince of the power of the air, the spirit that is now at work in the sons of disobedience—among whom we all once lived in the passions of our flesh, carrying out the desires of the body and the mind, and were by nature children of wrath, like the rest of mankind. But God, being rich in mercy, because of the great love with which he loved us, even when we were dead in our trespasses, made us alive together with Christ—by grace you have been saved—and raised us up with him and seated us with him in the heavenly places in Christ Jesus, so that in the coming ages he might show the immeasurable riches of his grace in kindness toward us in Christ Jesus. For by grace you have been saved through faith. And this is not your own doing; it is the gift of God, not a result of works, so that no one may boast. ***For we are his workmanship, created in Christ Jesus for good works, which God prepared beforehand, that we should walk in them."***
(Ephesians 2:1-10)

Tennis is the single greatest sport on the planet. Hands down. If you disagree, well then your wrong... yeah, that's right...you want a piece of me? Don't make me hit you in the head with my racquet! (This is what happens when an Iranian plays tennis!)

I grew up playing tennis. When I was twelve, my friends and I would get up on weekend and summer mornings and play an average of five hours a day. I still try to get to the racquet club as much as I can.

My favorite tennis player these days is Andy Roddick, a former number one player in the world. For many years, Andy has held the record for the fastest serve in tennis history. As a matter of fact, he keeps breaking his own record. The last serve was clocked at 155 miles-per-hour. This may come as a shock to some, but Andy and I have a lot in common. We both play with the same kind of racquet. Sure, he has an endorsement deal, and I have to pay for mine, but that is beside the point. We also wear the same kind of shoes when we hit the courts. Sure, he gets paid for wearing his, and I have to pay to wear mine, but that's beside the point. We both use the same kind of strings. They are made of a blend of catgut and fibers that are woven together. (Proof that there actually is a real purpose for the cat—just kidding.) We're both big serve guys. Some people say that our service motions even look the same. I have actually studied Andy's serve in slow motion. You can dissect it frame by frame on the Web. On average, Andy will ace his opponent five-seven times in a match, and so do I. Sure, he aces professionals, and I generally ace senior citizens and little kids, but that's beside the point.

The point is, in all seriousness, I will never be able to serve like Andy Roddick. I can mimic his service moves, wear the same outfit, use the same racquet, and even change my name to his, but it still won't work. All my work will not work. I am not Andy Roddick. Now, suppose for the sake of illustration, I was able to ask Andy Roddick to live in me. What if I could get Andy to take complete control of my life? I know it's a weird thought, but think about it. If Andy Roddick lived in me, then all I would have to do in order to serve like Andy would be to let him serve through me. It wouldn't actually be me serving, but Andy serving through me. I wouldn't be doing things (work) *like* him trying to achieve his power and control; I would already have his power and control since he would be in me. I would then let him display *his* power through *me*. That describes the true Christian life.

Some consider the Christian life to be about behavior modification. New believers understand that they are saved to do God's good work. However, using their own strength, failure comes; so they try even harder. Living life this way is exhausting. Decent results may come, but only within human means. Eventually, the new believer is worn out from all the hard work and inconsistent results, and gives up.

The grace-filled Christian life, however, is not about working hard to be like Jesus. It is about Jesus living in and doing his good work through us. This lifestyle is echoed in the old saying, "Let go, and let God."

Christianity is much more than a changed life; it's the exchanged life. It's not about behavior changing, but about identity changing. It's not about work, but about *worth* in Christ. Do you see it?

In Ephesians 2:9, Paul reminds us that we are saved apart from works. However, right after that, in verse ten, he reinforces the fact that although we are saved apart from works, there is much work to be done. So much work that we cannot possibly do it all on our own, no matter how hard we try. The good news is that we don't have to do it all. He wants to do it through us. It's his will that he wants to accomplish—he just allows us to be a part of it. As God's masterpieces, he creates us for his purpose. In 2 Timothy 1:9, Paul says that when we are saved we are called to a holy calling. He goes on to say that this is not because of our works, but because of God's own purpose and grace. There is Kingdom work to be done. We are saved apart from works to do his good works. This is not about doing a bunch of Christian work so God will be happier with you. God is as pleased with you as he is ever going to be, because he is completely pleased with Christ, and Christ lives in you. The Christian life is about living in obedience because we are Christians. A cow doesn't moo so he can be a cow. He moos because he already is a cow. A duck quacks and an apple tree grows apples because that's *what they are*. They naturally *do* what they *are*. They don't *do* to *become*; they *do* because they already *are*. A cow, a duck, and an apple tree still have to grow. Spiritually speaking, so do you and I. As we grow in grace through the process of sanctification, we become more and more in our behavior what we have already become in our position. Sanctification is a process of growing, by faith, as God's new creations. Titus 2:1-4 reads, "For the grace of God has appeared, bringing salvation for all people [justification], training us to renounce ungodliness and worldly passions, and to live self-controlled, upright, and godly lives in the present age [sanctification], waiting for our blessed hope, the appearing of the glory of our great God and Savior Jesus Christ, who gave himself for us to redeem us from all lawlessness and to purify for himself a people for his own possession; who are zealous for good works [sanctification]."

In Ephesians 2:1-4, Paul reminds us of who we were before we were in Christ; who we were in our own works, both good and bad.

In Ephesians 2:4-9, Paul reminds us of who we become when we are in Christ; who we are, not by our works, either good nor bad.

In Ephesians 2:10, Paul reminds us how we are to live since we are in Christ. We're not to live by our own works. Saved apart from good works to do his good works. Verse 10 complements verses 1-9. Verse 10 is the natural overflow of what happens when verses 4-9 become a reality in us.

Another way to look at it is to say that verse 10 is about our *responsibility* as Christians to live holy lives. Paul is saying that since we're masterpieces, we should act like it. Be the masterpiece that you are. I once heard Dr. Adrian Rogers on the radio give an amazing, biblical definition of responsibility. He defined responsibility as our response to God's ability. Wow! That makes beautiful sense. Like the Andy Roddick illustration, instead of trying to mimic the behavior of Christ, as believers we give ourselves to God and say, "I can't do it, but you can through me. I want to respond not in my own ability, but in yours." This turns our actions from legalistic "doing" to grace-filled "being." Our acts of righteousness should be done in the strength of God's grace and not by our own sheer determination. Some of us may even need to repent of our own acts of self-righteousness.

In the last part of verse 10, we find tremendous comfort in knowing that not only does God call us to live holy, responsible lives, but he also tells us that this life is a path already set before us. God has predetermined the works he wants to do in and through us. These works are spelled out all over the Bible. From the fruit of the Spirit, to the Beatitudes, to the Great Commission, God is very clear about the particular works he wants to display through our lives. *The Expositor's Bible Commentary* explains Ephesians 2:10: "The life of goodness that regeneration produces has been prepared for believers to walk about in for all eternity. The road is already built. Here is a further reason why the Christian has nothing left to boast about. Even the good he now does has its source in God, who has made it possible."[1]

Be still. Listen to what God is saying to you.

1. What is the biggest difference between doing works to be a Christian and doing works because you already are a Christian?

   How does this, when applied to our behavior, look the same while being so different?

2. How does Ephesians 2:10 complement Ephesians 2:1-9 and not contradict it?

3. What is the point of the Andy Roddick illustration as it pertains to the Christian life?

4. How was *responsibility* defined in today's devotional?

Lord, I thank you that today your grace is *comforting* me in these areas:

Lord, I thank you that today your grace is *convicting* me in these areas:

Lord, I thank you that today your grace is *calling* me to:

Today's Memory Verses: Ephesians 2:1-10

Portrait of Grace

____

fill in your name

As the last day of this journey, I want to end with a very personal Portrait of Grace. So personal, in fact, that it is actually going to be about *you*. I even want you to put your name in the blank as the title of this portrait. Throughout the Portraits of Grace ordinary people, in extraordinary circumstances, have been portrayed as masterpieces proclaiming the glory of God. These people are no different than you and me. In fact, as believers, we are each God's very own "portrait of grace." No matter what our circumstances—usual or unusual, harsh or easy—we can reflect God's glory as we live in his grace.

Here are a few things to remember as you tell your story:

1. There is no such thing as a boring testimony. You don't have to be a supermodel with HIV or someone who was pardoned by a judge to have a story to tell. If our stories were all about us, that would be one thing. But our stories are ultimately about God. A story about an ordinary life in the hands of an extraordinary God is always worth hearing. That's what makes every testimony of grace worth telling.

2. We are all portraits in progress. Until the day we go to heaven, God is continuously creating in us and through us. If you're going through a dark time in your life right now, know that the Master Artist has not yet finished the painting.

3. Remember that this is not about getting glory. This is about giving God the glory. Write with a heart full of thankfulness and gratitude. Make much of him. Not just in the next few pages, but for the rest of your life.

Now, go ahead. Take out your mental video camera and press rewind. With a heart of worship, think about God's brush strokes in your life. See how he has worked to create a masterpiece with you. Take the next few pages and write your story. Remember his graciousness to you as you seek to make much of the ultimate "Grace Extender."

My portrait

Meet the author

In 1979 Iran was embroiled in a bitter revolution. Untold numbers of people were slaughtered everyday. Gas prices skyrocketed. Fear and panic gripped the Mid East. Fortunately, in the midst of this horrible turmoil, God was moving.

Leaving everything behind, nine-year-old David and his family were forced to escape their native homeland of Iran hoping to begin a new life in the vastly different culture of the United States. The following years, found a young and isolated David Nasser seeking and trying everything imaginable to be accepted, but was always left the outsider. Eventually, David found true acceptance at the age of eighteen, when through the persistent witness of a body of believers, David received salvation and purpose through a deep and personal relationship with Jesus Christ.

As one of the nation's forefront speakers and visionaries, God has blessed David with the ability to reach the high tech, attention-lacking culture of Generation Next. Involved in revivals, citywide rallies, camps, and school assemblies, David speaks to over 700,000 people each year. The heart's cry of D. Nasser Outreach is to effectively present the same relevant message, the Gospel of Christ, using fresh, innovative methods and resources. Alongside his own full time ministry, DNO is also growing rapidly as a mentoring and consulting ministry. DNO has worked extensively with ministries such as BGEA, Youth Specialties, Student Life, Acquire the Fire, and many others. David, his wife Jennifer and their children live in Alabama.

Notes

6

1. Randy Alcorn, The Grace and Truth Paradox (Sisters, OR: Multnomah [Publishers, Inc.], 2003).

7

1. Steve McVey, Grace Walk (Eugene, OR: Harvest House [Publishers], 1995).
2. Brennan Manning, The Ragamuffin Gospel (Sisters, OR: Multnomah [Publishers, Inc.], 1990).

9

1. Wayne Grudem, Systematic Theology (Grand Rapids, MI: Zondervan, 1994).
2. Watchman Nee, The Normal Christian Life (n.p.: Tyndale House[Publishers], 1977).

10

1. "Come Bite Me!" Right...Wednesday, November 3, 2004, www.rueters.com.

11

1. R.C. Sproul, Saved From What? (Wheaton, IL: Crossway Books, 2002).

13

1. John Newton, "Amazing Grace," Then Sings My Soul (Robert J. Morgan) (Nashville, TN: Thomas Nelson [Publishers], 2003).

14

1. Frederick William Faber, "There's A Wideness in God's Mercy" (written 1862).
2. Randy Alcorn, The Grace and Truth Paradox.
3. Stormie Omartian, Finding Peace for Your Heart (Nashville, TN: Thomas Nelson [Publishers, Inc.], 1991).

15

1. Bill Gillham, Lifetime Guarantee (Eugene, OR: Harvest House [Publishers], 1993).

16

1. Randy Alcorn, The Treasure Principle (Sisters, OR: Multnomah [Publishers, Inc.],

17

1. Ray Comfort, Hell's Best Kept Secret (Springdale, PA: Whitaker House, 1989).

18

1. Michael Card, A Violent Grace (Sisters, OR: Multnomah [Publishers, Inc.], 2000).
2. Isaac Watts, "When I Survey the Wondrous Cross," Then Sings My Soul (Robert J. Morgan) (Nashville, TN: Thomas Nelson [Publishers], 2003).

19

1. Charles Wesley, "O for a Thousand Tongues to Sing," (written 1739, copyright: Public Domain).

22

1. Martin Nystrum, "Your Grace is Sufficient" (n.p.: Integrity's Hosanna! Music/ ASCAP, 1991).

23

1. Newton, "Amazing Grace."

25

1. Charles Spurgeon, "Believers Tested by Trials," Spurgeon Expository Encyclopedia, 14 vols. (n.p.: Baker Book House, 1952), 14.
2. Horatio Spafford, "It Is Well With My Soul," Then Sings My Soul (Robert J. Morgan) (Nashville, TN: Thomas Nelson [Publishers], 2003).

26

1. Grudem, Systematic Theology.

27

1. J.I. Packer, Knowing God, 20th anniversary ed. (Nottingham, UK: InterVarsity Press, 1993).
2. Charles Spurgeon, "The Spirit of Bondage and Adoption," Spurgeon Expository Encyclopedia., 14 vols. (n.p.: Baker Book House, 1952), 1.
3. Mark Stibble, From Orphans to Heirs (Oxford, UK: Bible Reading Fellowship, 1999).

31

1. Jonathan Edwards, The Works of Jonathan Edwards, 1 vols. (n.p., UK: Banner of Truth Trust, 1979), 1.
2. Rick Warren, The Purpose Driven Life (Grand Rapids, MI: Zondervan [Publishing Company], 2002).

33

1. Tony Evans, Free At Last (Chicago, IL: Moody Press, 2001).
2. Charles Spurgeon, Spurgeon Expository Encyclopedia, 14 vols. (n.p.: Baker Book House, 1952), 14.

34

1. John Piper, The Godward Life (Sisters, OR: Multnomah [Publishers, Inc.], 1997.
2. Charles Swindoll, The Grace Awakening (Nashville, TN: W Publishing Group, 2003).

37

1. Randy Alcorn, The Grace and Truth Paradox
2. C.S. Lewis, The Lion, the Witch, and the Wardrobe (n.p., UK: Harper Collins [Publishers], 1994).

38

1. Frank E. Gaebelein, The Expositor's Bible Commentary, 12 vols. (Grand Rapids, MI: Zondervan [Publishing Company], 1978), 11.

Portrait of Grace, Pardoned

1. Julia Johnston, "Grace Greater than Our Sin" (n.p.: Hope [Publishing Company], 1910, renewed 1938).

All Scripture quoted is taken from the English Standard Version unless otherwise noted.